LOS
ANGELES

A pocket guide to the city's best
cultural hangouts, shops, bars
and eateries

ANDREA BLACK

Hardie Grant

TRAVEL

CONTENT/

INTRODUCTION

In Los Angeles, anything is possible. Yes, the bulk of the entertainment industry is based here, and along with that are all the dreamers who are wanting their bit part in this world, but this is not what makes Los Angeles great.

Beyond the blockbuster billboards, you'll find highly walkable precincts offering new discoveries around every corner. In multi-ethnic LA, family-run taqueria stands thrive next to dumpling houses, Jewish delis and sushi restaurants. Chicken and waffle houses abut fresh fruit vendor carts, and Korean, Thai and Armenian gastronomical delights can be found within the one strip mall.

It's also an eminently photogenic city. There's an abundance of art, museums and incredible design. Los Angeles' streetscapes are a product of the curbside driving culture of the 1950s and 1960s when architecture was used to attract drivers to their businesses. Everywhere there are diners, carwashes and motels still in operation, where you can appreciate this bright mid-century design, flanked by palm trees, of course. And natural beauty is right nearby, with stunning beaches for swimming, surfing and seeing the sunset. There's incredible walks where squirrels frolic, coyotes howl, birds sing and mountain lions roam (it's true!). Spend an afternoon hiking the hills and then as night falls look down upon the twinkling city, so quiet from afar. It's here you will likely fall in love with LA. I did.

But first a confession. On my first visit to the City of Angels, I was overwhelmed. The reason? I didn't have a plan. That famous quote that 'Los Angeles is 72 suburbs in search of a city' rang true. It was the days before Uber/Lyft and decent public transport (it's now a lot easier to get around since the Metro train lines were introduced) and I had made the rookie mistake of not hiring a car. I now know that LA is a city you have to discover village by village, and splitting it into precincts and spending time in each is the best way. They all offer something different. It's now up there as my favourite city in the world, with each stay yielding new surprises. I just wish I had this book back when I first visited.

Andrea Black

A PERFECT LO/ ANGELE/ DAY

How do you spend a day in this sprawling city? You can choose the sun, sand and surf of the beach precincts, the shopping and eating delights of West Hollywood or Los Feliz, explore nature trails in Griffith Park, but here I've chosen the inner-city experience of Downtown.

I'm not usually into eggs, but I'd line up for **Eggslut** in the **Grand Central Market** any day to power up for the day. It's aptly named, with customers always coming back for more of the addictive fluffy eggs, chives, cheddar, caramelised onions and Sriracha mayonnaise on a warm brioche bun. I'd then check out the modern artworks and take a few pics along the way at **The Broad** museum, though I'd make sure I had a timeslot booked in beforehand, otherwise the queues can be brutal. Afterwards I'd head across the road to the **Museum of Contemporary Art (MOCA)** to view the expressive use of colour in the roomful of Mark Rothkos. Retail therapy awaits so I'd browse **Downtown LA's boutiques**, full of men's and women's fashion and pick up a small keepsake in a homewares store.

Time for a late lunch, I'd look for a taco truck or perhaps pop into **Guisados** for a mole poblano taco. I'd then head to the **Los Angeles Public Library** and take a tour of the historic building, along the way I'd spot incredible **murals** that fill Downtown. Come late afternoon, I'd stop by **Clifton's** cafeteria for a cocktail, an LA institution since 1935. There are five bars here to choose from amongst the nature dioramas and taxidermied beasts (if it offends, avoid). Writer Jack Kerouac wrote about it in *On the Road*. I might then see if I can go and buy a first edition of said book at **The Last Bookstore** right around the corner. I'd peruse the shelves while listening to an author event.

Then I'd head to the **Imperial Western Beer Company** housed at Union Station and see the last of the day's sunlight stream in, highlighting the intricately restored soaring Art Deco ceiling. I'd walk across to **Philippe** for a French dipped sandwich amongst the sawdust covered room. I'd then step out to look out at Downtown, surveying all the landmarks explored and then plot my next day in the City of Angels.

POCKET TOP PICKS

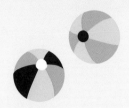

INSPIRING ARCHITECTURE

BEST DRINKS

TOP UNIQUELY LA EXPERIENCES

BEST OLD SCHOOL LA

TOP CHEAP EATS

BEST VIEWS

TOP SHOPPING

BEST CHANCE OF A CELEBRITY SIGHTING

BEST DINERS AND DIVES

BEST MUSEUMS AND GALLERIES

LOS ANGELES OVERVIEW

SAN
FERNANDO

SAN
FERNANDO
VALLEY

13

PRECINCT*S*

FIELD TRIP*S*

WESTSIDE

SANTA
MONICA

4

*Santa
Monica
Bay*

(10)

BURBANK

VERDUGOS

(14)

(9)

GLENDALE

PASADENA

(8)

(2)

NORTHEAST
L.A.

EL MONTE

(1)

(3)

CENTRAL
L.A.

(7)

(5)

(6)

EASTSIDE

LOS
ANGELES

(12)

SOUTH
L.A.

INGLEWOOD

DOWNEY

SOUTHEAST

NORWALK

SOUTH
BAY

TORRANCE

(11)

HOLLYWOOD

Forget what you've heard about busloads of tourists, big-brand shopping and celebrity lookalikes and superheroes hawking for photos outside Grauman's Chinese Theatre, as Hollywood is finally changing for the better. That famous giant Hollywood sign up in the hills has always been a beacon, and now underneath, along Hollywood Boulevard, Vine Street and Sunset Boulevard, is a slew of new restaurants and bars making this a must-visit precinct for both tourists and local Angelenos. There are some worthy stayers too, classic fare at Musso & Frank Grill (*see* p. 8), which featured in Quentin Tarantino's *Once Upon a Time in Hollywood*, is well-worth making an advance booking for, as well as a night at the only-in-LA Magic Castle (*see* p. 5).

Of course, this is Tinseltown central and the legend (more of a mindset than a destination) that is Hollywood lives on, so there will always be some celebrity element to any visit, from the more than 2600 five-pointed terrazzo stars that make up the Walk of Fame (*see* p. 4) to the dearly departed at the Hollywood Forever Cemetery (*see* p. 2).

Getting to Hollywood without a car is easy too with the $8 FlyAway service (*see* p. 140) from LAX and the Red Metro Line from Downtown.

→ *The Hollywood sign, built to advertise a real estate development in 1923, looms large*

1 HOLLYWOOD FOREVER CEMETERY

6000 Santa Monica Blvd
323 469 1181
Mon–Fri 8.30am–5pm, Sat–Sun 8.30am–4.30pm
Weekly events 7.30–11.30pm
[MAP p. 151 E3]

It may be a cemetery but Hollywood Forever is also a venue, outdoor cinema and cultural space. Part of the appeal is the calibre of those eternally resting here. By day, entry is free (maps featuring locations of graves are $5). Stroll the gardens and pay respects to famous residents, including Judy Garland, Rudolph Valentino, Cecil B. DeMille, Don Adams, Chris Cornell from Soundgarden and two Ramones (Johnny and Dee Dee). Judging by the discreetly placed (and rather formidable) security guards dotted around the grounds, it won't go too well if you rock up with a six pack of beers looking to party with the Ramones. The grounds are immaculate, with tree-lined walkways, an abundance of lawn and the odd peacock strutting about. It makes the perfect setting for night-time events, which include screenings of classic movies and outdoor shows by big-name music acts. Book ahead for events.

POCKET TIP

Plan your visit to be in early November for the US's largest Dia de Los Muertos (Day of the Dead) celebration.

POCKET TIP

Nothing says summer in LA like an outdoor concert at the legendary Hollywood Bowl. There is usually an act to suit every taste on its summer concert schedule but get in quick as most sell out.

2 ESOTOURIC TRUE CRIME TOURS

Various meeting points & tours

Considering a bus tour to learn more about Hollywood and LA as a whole? Choose this. Yes, it leans toward the dark side but it's guaranteed to be more entertaining than any tours that drive past gated mansions of celebrities. Esotouric's most popular is the Real Black Dahlia Crime bus tour, a still unsolved brutal murder from 1947 that has been the subject of endless books, podcasts and documentaries. On this tour you'll explore the last weeks of Elizabeth Short's life by visiting the lobby of the Biltmore Hotel in Downtown LA, the Greyhound bus station where she checked her bags and then the site in Leimert Park where her bisected body was discovered. The knowledgeable guides get in-depth on theories of what happened to this enigmatic black-haired beauty, a mystery that has gripped Angelenos for more than 70 years. Esotouric run other tours too, from Charles Manson to a Route 66 tour.

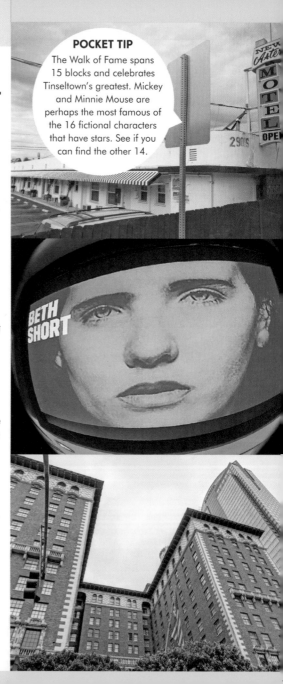

POCKET TIP
The Walk of Fame spans 15 blocks and celebrates Tinseltown's greatest. Mickey and Minnie Mouse are perhaps the most famous of the 16 fictional characters that have stars. See if you can find the other 14.

POCKET TIP

Keep an eye out for the Capitol Records Building as you drive along Highway 101. The tower looks like a stack of records, complete with a needle at the top blinking out 'Hollywood' in Morse code.

3 AMOEBA MU∫IC

6400 Sunset Blvd
323 245 6400
Mon–Sat 10.30am–11pm,
Sun 11am–10pm
[MAP p.151 D2]

If you're a music lover, your trip to Los Angeles won't be complete without a rummage through the racks at the world's largest independent record store. Beware, it can be intimidating at first, as the room is huge and every genre of music is represented. But don't be overwhelmed, as sections are well-labelled and staff is there to help. Want to know what to listen to? Amoeba releases a handy guide called Music We Like on what they are digging right now. Even if you don't usually invest in rare vinyl or music books and ephemera, it's worth dropping into this store to see who might be playing instore. On any given week you might see Sia, Courtney Barnett or Paul McCartney. Check online for the schedule.

4 HOLLYWOOD FARMERS' MARKET

Cnr Ivar Ave & Selma Ave
Sun 8am–1pm
[MAP p.151 D2]

Every Sunday, the very heart of Hollywood transforms into one of the best farmers' markets in the city, with vendors from all over Southern California selling an array of organic produce and artisanal comestibles. You'll find locally grown fruit and vegetables from long-time tenants. Don't be surprised to see the likes of Natalie Portman picking through the array of goodies. Locals swear by wild salmon, which is line-caught off the coast by **J & P Seafood** that very morning and **Aged Butchery** provide an excellent array of ethically farmed meat. There's queues for the terrific tamales from **Tamales, Treats and More**, choice local goat's cheese from **Drake's Family Farm** and the line for **Bub and Grandma's** bakery is already snaking down the road at 8.30am. If you're staying in a self-catered apartment in Hollywood then this is a great place to stock the fridge.

POCKET TIP
The Cinerama Dome on Sunset is the place to see 70mm first-run hits with incredible sound. This famous theatre also hosts screenings of cult classics and vintage blockbusters.

5 MAGIC CAJTLE

7001 Franklin Ave
323 851 3313
Mon–Fri 5pm–2am, Sat–Sun
10am–3pm, 5pm–2am
[MAP p. 150 B1]

Whisper the words 'open sesame' to a golden owl and a bookcase opens to reveal the glory of The Magic Castle, a private club for members of the Academy of Magical Arts that, over the years, has counted Cary Grant, Tippi Hedren and Ryan Gosling as visitors and members. Neil Patrick Harris was recently the president. It may be private but there are ways to get in without knowing a member – simply stay at the Magic Castle Hotel next door or stay at a Hilton, who have recently become partners. Housed in an ornately decorated Victorian mansion steps away from Hollywood Boulevard, inside there are rooms dedicated to card tricks and elaborate illusions. Part of the experience is the dinner beforehand, where they conjure up a good steak and seafood. It's not your everyday dining destination but if you want an unusual and memorable experience then be sure to book ahead, as it's Hollywood's best-kept secret. There is a strict dress code: a coat and tie or fancy frock are obligatory. A rabbit in a top hat? Optional.

6 MUSSO & FRANK GRILL

6667 Hollywood Blvd
323 467 7788
Tues–Sat 11am–11pm,
Sun 4–9pm
[MAP p. 150 C2]

Don't be put off by its address right in the thick of tourist-central on Hollywood Boulevard, Musso & Frank is well worth braving the teeming hordes and superman impersonators for. Serving classic American fare since 1919, this stalwart has always been a magnet for actors and writers. In the past century you could have shared a seat at the mahogany bar with Marilyn Monroe, Leonardo DiCaprio, Ernest Hemingway or Charles Bukowski. You won't find any foams or fusion here; these classics have been on the menu since opening – from shrimp cocktails to enormous rib-eye steaks cooked perfectly to order. And it's not overly pricey, main meals begin at $25. The wait staff are of the wisecracking variety who work the tables like it's all an act, and we know it, but in this nocturnal, walnut-panelled and leather boothed realm it seems to make perfect sense. Book ahead as it's still riding the wave after featuring in Tarantino's *Once Upon a Time in Hollywood*.

POCKET TIP

In-N-Out Burger's (7009 Sunset Blvd) secret menu is popular amongst those in the know. Ask for your burger 'Animal Style' and it will come with extra pickles, dressing and your patty 'mustard grilled'.

7 APL BBQ

1680 Vine St
323 416 1280
Tues–Sat 11.30am–3pm
[MAP p. 151 D2]

By night, APL is one of Hollywood's foremost steak restaurants offering a high-end experience at a high-end price. But by day this ornate room (think leather banquettes, white marble tables and an abundance of antique mirrors) becomes a purveyor of authentic Southern-style barbecue in a much more wallet-friendly manner. Feast on mountains of superbly cooked brisket, pork ribs and pulled pork overseen by chef Adam Perry Lang, a celebrated Barbecue Hall of Fame pit-master. Authentic sides and serious barbecue sandwiches (try the burnt ends sandwich) round out the menu and there's local craft beers on tap (or in cans), should you need a little tipple to accompany your meal. If you're planning a walk around Hollywood then this is easily one of the best lunches you can get for the price.

8 GOOD TIME/ AT DAVEY WAYNE'/

1611 N El Centro Ave
323 962 3804
Mon–Fri 5pm–2am,
Sat–Sun 2pm–2am
[MAP p. 151 D2]

Sure, it may look like you're stepping off the streets of Hollywood into a backyard garage sale straight out of the 1970s but that's all part of the charm at this casual bar. Named after their late father, David Wayne Houston, a blue-collar pool shark who enjoyed late nights in his garage building and fixing things, his twin sons decided to design a bar as a tribute to him and to all who have lost their dads. Beyond that garage (you enter via a refrigerator door) is a mid-century-style living room with wood-panelling, an abundance of velvet and an outdoor area complete with a caravan selling snow-cones and tiki cocktails. The vibe is definitely laid-back, think *The Partridge Family*, complete with a '70s soundtrack. Order the Some People Call Me Maurice cocktail with crème de menthe, crème de cacao and straight-up cream. Cue the wolf whistle.

9 HARVARD AND ∫TONE

5221 Hollywood Blvd
747 231 0699
Mon–Sun 8pm–2am
[MAP p. 156 A2]

Harvard and Stone is a rare Hollywood beast; a friendly spot with a local rock club vibe. How about some cool tunes, cheap beers and a quality cocktail list to go with that? The R&D bar, so named for its ever-rotating cocktail menu, sits in between the music room and a dark wood-panelled lounge area in the back. It plays host to a variety of local rock acts with a burlesque show every Saturday night. The scene is mostly young (ish) rock fans with an air of gothic decadence. In between bands the DJ is pumping out a playlist of records; some punk, glam and classic rock. If the music's not your thing then there are plenty of nooks and crannies with deep, leather couches in which to camp for a tête-à-tête.

11

SILVER LAKE & LOS FELIZ

With verdant hills ripe for urban hikes, lakes (real and man-made), some of Los Angeles' widest variety of restaurants, bars and boutiques, Silver Lake and Los Feliz pretty much have it all, and more. When the area started gentrifying in the late 1990s, creative types began opening interesting stores and restaurants. Fast-forward 20 years later, and while the real estate prices are quite a bit higher, there are still incredible eateries, bars, markets, and a glut of design and fashion and homewares stores to explore.

It's not surprising that this is the area that wealthy hip celebrities, professionals and an ever-increasing number of families are moving into. Plus, the precinct is an architecture lover's dream, with homes by Frank Lloyd Wright and other modernists that followed him. Don't miss his Hollyhock House (see p. 15). Griffith Park (see p. 14), with its range of hikes and, by night, twinkling lights and silence is right here, too.

This is an area where you really don't need a car, you can walk, if you're willing to go the distance ... there's always an Uber or Lyft at the end of the night.

→ *Hiking Griffith Park affords incredible views of Los Angeles*

SIGHTS
1. Griffith Park Observatory
2. Hollyhock House

SHOPPING
3. Lake
4. Soap Plant/Wacko
5. Bar Keeper

EATING
6. Magpies Softserve
7. Little Dom's
8. Botanica

EATING & DRINKING
9. Zebulon
10. Dresden

1 GRIFFITH PARK OBSERVATORY

2800 East Observatory Rd,
Los Feliz
213 473 0800
Tues–Fri 12pm–10pm,
Sat–Sun 10am–10pm
[MAP p.156 A1]

There's only one place to see the bright lights of Tinseltown and the cosmos – at the Griffith Park Observatory. We've seen it in movies from *Rebel Without A Cause* to *La La Land*. It's free to enter and you can look through telescopes across to the Hollywood sign, as well as explore exhibits and see live shows in the **Samuel Oschin Planetarium**. On selected Saturdays, **Los Angeles Astronomical Society** volunteers hold parties and help teach you about the stars in the sky. Try one of the trails at Griffith Park and hike up there – you'll spot horses and lots of dogs (being walked by their owners) along the way and hawks up above. You'll probably spot a celebrity or two as well, as the walk is a popular daily fitness ritual. Parking is limited so best to hike up from the base.

POCKET TIP

Hidden amongst the walking tracks around Griffith Park is the Old Los Angeles Zoo, which was founded in 1902 and finally closed in 1965 leaving behind ruins of old enclosures and a picnic area.

2 HOLLYHOCK HOU/E

4800 Hollywood Blvd, Los Feliz
323 988 0516
Thurs–Sun 11am–4pm
[MAP p. 156 B2]

Recently announced as Los Angeles' first UNESCO World Heritage Site, architect Frank Lloyd Wright's ode to California was built between 1919 and 1921 on a hill in East Hollywood. It is named for motifs of the hollyhock flower that dominate the concrete house's exterior. Hollyhock House was owned by oil heiress, Aline Barnsdall, who never lived in it and instead donated the home and the surrounding grounds to the City of Los Angeles in 1927. You can look at it from afar for free but it's worth shelling out the $7 for a 45-minute docent-led tour of the house. Sure, you have to don protective booties but you'll get to see the intricate hollyhock designs, as well as custom-made rugs and textiles made for Barnsdall by Wright. Advance bookings are required by phone or online (www.barnsdall.org/hollyhock-house).

POCKET TIP

Every Friday from the end of May to August there's an evening of wine-tasting, music and food trucks outside the house in the grounds of Barnsdall Art Park.

3 LAKE

1618 1/2 Silver Lake Blvd,
Silver Lake
323 664 6522
Sun–Mon 11am–6pm,
Tues–Sat 11am–6.30pm
[MAP p.156 C3]

If you want to get a sense of how an LA creative cool woman might dress, then you should head to Lake, and aim straight for the sales rack. The curated collection features Cali casual wear like kaftans, rompers, hemp fabric tees and linen shorts. Accessories abound throughout with straw hats, baskets, scarves and a range of jewellery from local makers. Special mention should go to the block prints it sells by local designers Block Shop Textiles, worth rolling up in a tube and posting home. There's also a great apothecary range with some sustainable local brands represented, such as the heavenly Litoralle Aromatica. What's great about Lake is that even if you're not one of the Cali chic, the staff won't make you feel like you've accidentally stumbled into the wrong shop. They love a chat.

POCKET TIP

Just across the road is supercool Hemingway and Sons, a menswear store stocking curated casualwear, shoes, caps, homewares and apothecary. The sales rack is the first port of call with deep discounts offered.

PLEASE USE SAMPLE TESTERS. DO NOT OPEN SEALED JARS.

GEL/BODY OIL CAN BE CUSTOM SCENTED! BOTTLES ON FLOOR UNSCENTED. SAMPLES LOCATED IN MIDDLE COUNTER

4 SOAP PLANT/ WACKO

4633 Hollywood Blvd, Los Feliz
323 663 0122
Mon–Wed 11am–7pm,
Thurs 11am–9pm,
Fri–Sat 11am–10pm,
Sun 12pm–6pm
[MAP p. 156 B2]

A long-time magnet for pop-culture fans looking for products with a counter-cultural edge, the Soap Plant/Wacko's massive warehouse began in 1971 as Soap Plant. Owner Billy Shire and his mum Barbara wanted a place to sell her homemade soaps along with Billy's handmade leather garments. The punk era inspired Billy to expand the store to sell books, music, toys and posters with an eye towards alternative culture, adopting the Wacko name. They've been growing ever since and after moving to their current space in 1995 they added the **La Luz De Jesus Gallery** that displays art with an outsider edge. Wacko's shelves bulge with an incredible range of books, magazines, T-shirts, toys, games, records, posters, Mexican folk art and a full range of Barbara's beauty products.

POCKET TIP

Those in need of a coffee fix can find some decent options around Sunset Junction in Silver Lake, including Intelligentsia, Dinosaur and Roo; all offering top-notch artisanal blends.

17

5 BAR KEEPER

614 N Hoover St, Silver Lake
323 669 1675
Sun–Mon 11am–6pm,
Tues–Thurs 11am–7pm,
Fri–Sat 11am–8pm
[MAP p. 156 B3]

Angelenos take their cocktails
seriously and at Bar Keeper
they uphold this tradition by
offering what they call 'the
ritual of drinking spirits',
with a retail focus on quality
ingredients and the right
tools for your home bar. The
sunny retail space on busy
Hoover Street is a cocktail
connoisseur's nirvana selling
a large range of barware,
glassware, rare and small batch
spirits and an astonishing
selection of bitters and syrups.
They host regular tastings of
unique small batch spirits,
such as Haitian rum and Swiss
absinthe. Bar Keeper's friendly
staff are knowledgeable and
eager to talk cocktails and
mixology. They also offer a
selection of gift boxes with
the ingredients for classic
cocktails, such as negronis
and martinis.

6 MAGPIEƧ ƧOFTƧERVE

2660 Griffith Park Blvd,
Silver Lake
323 486 7094
Sun–Thurs 11am–10pm,
Fri–Sat 11am–11pm
[MAP p. 156 C2]

It's easy to miss Magpies –
it's a small shop in a strip
mall across from a busy
intersection – but, once found,
you will return. Guaranteed.
Magpies offers handmade
soft serve made from scratch;
no powders or mixes here.
Owners Warren and Rose
Schwartz are both chefs (Rose
also has a chemistry degree
so there's a definite scientific
approach here) and they go
beyond the traditional servings
with chef-driven flavours,
such as horchata (non-dairy),
the Cuban coffee-flavoured
cortadito, and Yuzu honey, a
traditional Korean tea. Flavours
change daily, and on my last
visit a couple of the highlights
were red velvet cake and
brownie butter. An added
bonus? Most of the flavours
are vegan. All toppings are
made in-house as well. Try
the butterscotch rice krispies
or the chocolate-covered
honeycomb. More please!

7 LITTLE DOM'S

2128 Hillhurst Ave, Los Feliz
323 661 0055
Sun–Thurs 8am–3pm &
5.30–11pm, Fri–Sat 8am–3pm
& 5.30pm–12am
[MAP p.156 B1]

Three words: blueberry ricotta pancakes. If you can find a better version of these fluffy, fruity delights anywhere else in the world, please let me know! But breakfast/brunch is not all that this classic Italian eatery does well. There's good reason why this Los Feliz stalwart is perennially packed out (there's often a celeb or two from Jon Hamm to Ryan Gosling holding business meetings here, too); the homemade spaghetti and meatballs is al dente and woodfired pizzas are a delight. Plus, they have a great wine list and the decor is classic low-key LA, with booths, a salvaged dark-wood bar and outdoor seating. Head here for the fixed-price Monday supper, $18 for three courses.

POCKET TIP

A couple of blocks down on Hillhurst is one of LA's best natural wine stores, Lou Wine Shop. It hosts tastings on Fridays 6–8pm and Saturdays, 4–7pm.

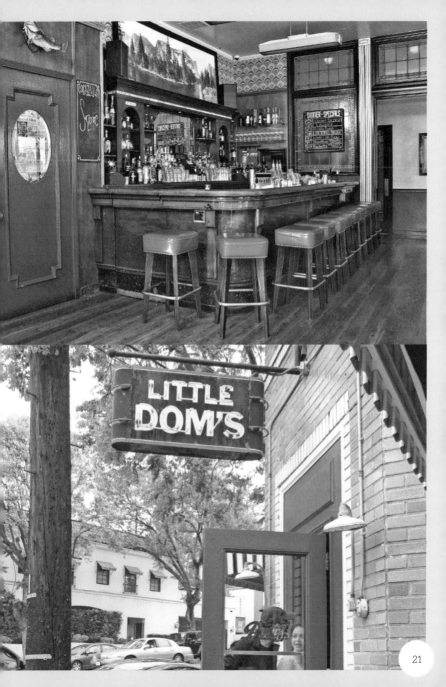

8 BOTANICA

1620 Silver Lake Blvd,
Silver Lake
323 522 6106
Sun–Thurs 9am–2pm &
5.30–10pm, Fri–Sat 9am–2pm
& 5.30–11pm
[MAP p. 156 C3]

There's good reason why the cuisine at all-day restaurant Botanica looks every bit as good as it tastes. Owners, Heather Sperling and Emily Fiffer, are former food editors and writers and they know how to style their menu to make it look amazing. Here, you'll find colour and flavour in every dish. Their greens are sourced from local farmers' markets and feature a rainbow of grains and herbacious garnishes. Their 'fattoush-y' salad of grilled and raw summer vegetables is a popular choice (to eat and to Instagram). Wicker and natural light dominate indoors but opt to sit in the outdoor garden setting amongst the verdant greenery. And don't just go for still or sparkling water, a truly refreshing choice is their arugula (rocket) lime aid, or maybe a glass of wine; natural wine, of course.

POCKET TIP

Got a hound at home that you're missing? Head over to the Silver Lake Reservoir and watch the dogs play in the dedicated fenced-off grounds. There's one for smaller dogs and another for larger breeds.

RESTAURANT + MARKET

COCKTAILS + NATURAL WINE

COFFEE + TEA

PRODUCE + PROVISIONS

+ MORE!

LIQUOR

9 ZEBULON

2478 Fletcher Dr, Los Feliz
323 663 6927
Mon–Fri 6pm–2am,
Sat 11am–2am, Sun 4pm–2am
[MAP p. 157 D2]

Sitting on the edge of Los Feliz, Frogtown, so called because it sits right on the Los Angeles River, is one of the latest up-and-coming areas in LA and Zebulon is its cultural hub. Originally opened in 2003 in Brooklyn, New York, the renowned alternative venue closed in 2012 before relocating to Los Angeles in 2017 (even the original 1930s wooden bar made the journey). Since then Zebulon has become one of LA's premier small venues. It not only hosts a range of obscure and emerging acts but also acting as a venue for secret shows from major artists, such as Questlove from The Roots and Cat Power. Zebulon's kitchen offers a simple menu that takes in bar favourites, such as burgers, small plates, sandwiches and salads and some quality vegetarian offerings. Even if you're not seeing a show, it's a great spot for a drink, a bite and to soak in the young and hip Frogtown vibe.

10 DRE/DEN

1760 N Vermont Ave, Los Feliz
323 665 4294
Tues–Sat 5pm–2am,
Sun–Mon 5pm–12am
[MAP p. 156 B2]

Slink into the curved white leather booths at Dresden in Los Feliz and it could be 1954, 1974 or 1994. Many would recognise the restaurant and bar from the movie *Swingers*. The same duo from the movie, Marty and Elayne Roberts, are still crooning Sinatra standards in the stone-walled lounge area; they've enjoyed decades of being the resident act here. Their biggest fans are seated around the piano scribbling requests on the napkins. Meanwhile in the dining room, suited waiters serve specialty prime ribs and pasta with Peach Melba for dessert. The 1960s Batman, Adam West, used to drop in here, and legend has it Ole Blue Eyes himself would stop by for a martini. Don't let the bland brick façade fool you – it's like walking into a dimly lit lounge bar directly from the '50s in the wee small hours.

WEST HOLLYWOOD

At less than five square kilometres, West Hollywood (sometimes shortened to WeHo) is a highly walkable city. A city? Yes, it's actually not officially part of Los Angeles, even though WeHo is right in amongst all the action in the heart of LA. This vibrant and inclusive city full of fashion and interior design stores was incorporated in 1984 when residents objected to Los Angeles County's plan to discontinue rent control. Biking here is encouraged, there's bike lanes (plus you can ride on the footpath/sidewalk) and there are numerous locations to hire bikes. West Hollywood also has a very high concentration of hotels, including The London, Sunset Marquis, The Andaz and Chateau Marmont. Nearly 40% of West Hollywood's population identifies as LGBTIQ+ and visitors are assured a safe, welcoming urban environment that was built on the needs and interests of the community. The LA Pride Festival in June and Halloween street party in October both draw hundreds of thousands of revellers, making them great times to visit. WeHo is home to incredible nightlife, from the world-famous Abbey Food and Bar (*see* p. 33) to rooftop views across the city at L.P. Rooftop Bar (*see* p. 34).

If you're tired of walking, the City of West Hollywood has a free shuttle service called The Sunset Trip on Friday and Saturday nights. Santa Monica Boulevard, famously known as Route 66, passes straight through West Hollywood. You can get your kicks on Route 66, then cycle or walk off the late night the next day.

→ *The famous Sunset Strip is in the heart of West Hollywood*

SIGHTS
1. Largo at the Coronet Comedy Club

SHOPPING
2. Book Soup
3. Pacific Design Center (PDC)

EATING
4. Mel's Drive-in Diner

EATING & DRINKING
5. Dan Tana's
6. The Abbey Food and Bar

DRINKING
7. L.P. Rooftop Bar
8. The Roger Room

1 LARGO AT THE CORONET COMEDY CLUB

366 N La Cienega Blvd
310 855 0350
Mon–Sun 6pm–11pm
[MAP p. 152 B4]

Comedy (and music) fans take note; before any LA trip it's essential to look at the line-up online at Largo – you may be surprised at the calibre of artist who plays this small room (capacity 130). There are strict rules to follow should you purchase tickets. When you arrive at Will Call box office to pick up the tickets on the night of the show, seats are then assigned first come first served, so if you want to sit closer, be sure to arrive early. Regulars are big names in comedy including Sarah Silverman, Tig Notaro and Zach Galifianakis. And a lot of the time they bring their famous comedian friends with them. Recently Jeff Garlin decided to bring his friend Larry David and they ended up on stage together for at least an hour, it was Curb Your Enthusiasm live!

2 BOOK SOUP

8818 Sunset Blvd
310 659 3110
Mon–Sat 9am–10pm,
Sun 9am–7pm
[MAP p. 152 A2]

This Sunset Strip bookshop, where the shelves are stacked to the ceiling is the go-to place in LA for small print-run, autographed and hard-to-find editions. Packed with a superb range of books (60,000 at last count), concentrating on art, film, photography, music and literary fiction, Book Soup host regular author events and signings by the likes of James Ellroy, Chuck Palahniuk and Annie Leibovitz. The knowledgeable staff are happy to answer questions, give tips or point you in the direction of a staff member who will specialise in a particular genre that you're interested in. It's this niche-driven attitude that makes Book Soup such a stand-out.

POCKET TIP

Barney's Beanery, a famous hangout for rockers from Jim Morrison to Marilyn Manson, is a casual bar and eatery on Route 66 that hasn't changed since the heyday of the Sunset Strip.

3 PACIFIC DE/IGN CENTER (PDC)

8687 Melrose Ave
310 657 0800
Mon–Fri 9am–5pm
[MAP p. 152 B3]

Looking to buy something inspiring for your own abode, or just want to see some seriously incredible design? This is the place to head in Los Angeles. First up, feast your eyes on the building itself. One wing is done out in red glass cladding, another in green, and then there's the building known as the 'blue whale' designed by Argentinian architect Cesar Pelli. Inside the PDC is 100 showrooms featuring 2200 luxury brands from Nate Berkus to Armani. It has the lot: furnishings, fabrics, wall and floor coverings. It's like being in a gallery or museum and even if you're not buying, you'll find plenty of ideas to use in your own home. If you are keen to buy, their Designer on Call and Buyer Referral Service can assist, simply book online (pacificdesigncenter.com). There are four **restaurants** at PDC (two are run by Wolfgang Puck), as well as a **theatre** and a satellite gallery of the **Museum of Contemporary Art (MOCA)**, see p. 62. There's parking onsite, too.

POCKET TIP
Stop in to browse the racks at Mary-Kate and Ashley Olsen's design store, The Row on Melrose Place.

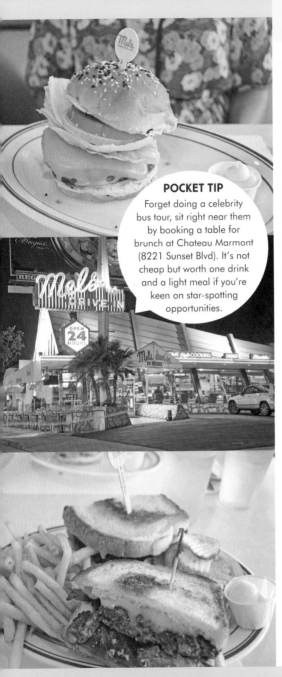

POCKET TIP

Forget doing a celebrity bus tour, sit right near them by booking a table for brunch at Chateau Marmont (8221 Sunset Blvd). It's not cheap but worth one drink and a light meal if you're keen on star-spotting opportunities.

4 MEL'S DRIVE-IN DINER

8585 Sunset Blvd
310 854 7201
Mon–Sun 24 hrs
[MAP p. 152 B2]

This diner is housed in a piece of LA pop culture history; an original piece of 'Googie' architecture, with sleek futuristic lines designed for the emerging car culture of the mid-20th century. Originally known as Ben Franks, from the 1960s to the 1980s this was the spot for young Sunset Strip groovers and rock stars, such as Frank Zappa, the Rolling Stones and Guns N' Roses, to hang post-show. In 1997, it became Mel's Drive-in but retains the mid-century charm of its predecessor, with juke boxes packed full of oldies tunes at every booth and a great menu of classic diner food including a killer cheeseburger. The walls are lined with pictures of the famous (and infamous) who've visited. If you want to feel like you're in the heady days of the Sunset Strip, Mel's is the place to go, plus it's open 24 hours. Even though it's called a drive-in, you don't need a car to visit.

31

5 DAN TANA'S

9071 Santa Monica Blvd
310 275 9444
Mon–Sat 5pm–1am,
Sun 5pm–12.30am
[MAP p. 152 A3]

When a bartender has been in an establishment for 50 years, you know it's worth stopping in for a toast. There's good reason why, as over the years Joni Mitchell, The Eagles and Clint Eastwood have ordered their martinis from Mike Gotovac at this classic Italian restaurant. He makes strong martinis and adds charisma to any conversation. The late Harry Dean Stanton had his own stool here. But Mike doesn't just save his A-game for the celebrities, on a recent visit after a long chat I was treated to a champagne on the house. Play your cards right and you might too. Either way, when you grab a bar stool and bend an elbow, you're in for a great night's entertainment. They also serve a great homemade lasagna here, which is just what's needed to soak up the cocktails.

6 THE ABBEY FOOD AND BAR

696 N Robertson Blvd
310 289 8410
Mon–Sun 12pm–2am
[MAP p. 152 A3]

Twice voted the best gay bar not just in LA but in the world, The Abbey has a reputation to uphold and it lives up to all the promises. Don't trust us? Let the people speak. The Abbey and Chapel are the No. 1 Uber and Lyft drop-off and pick-up locations for a nightclub or bar in the country. On a recent visit on a Tuesday night the place was packed, dancefloors were filled with dancers loving the hits of the '90s (admittedly it was '90s night). In the **Chapel**, a branch of The Abbey right next door, you'll hear EDM. Owner Todd Barnes describes The Abbey as a 'gay Disneyland', complete with lights, music and dancers. The food ain't bad either – think comfort staples like burgers and salads. There's outdoor patio booths to relax in after a session on the dance floor.

POCKET TIP

ONE Archives is the biggest collection of LGBTIQ+ materials in the world. Its ONE Gallery plays host to an ever-changing schedule of exhibits.

7 L.P. ROOFTOP BAR

603 N La Cienega Blvd
310 855 9955
Mon–Fri 5pm–2am,
Sat–Sun 12pm–2am
[MAP p. 152 B3]

This is where LA's beautiful people head for a sunset or late-night drink. Think greenery, incredible views across the Hollywood Hills and an open firepit and best of all – it's all al fresco. It's also surprisingly super-casual, so while the next table are all living their best life taking selfies, you can go about your own business of enjoying a cocktail (available by the glass or the pitcher), and that view of the Hollywood Hills. The owners are Australian hospitality giants Grant Smillie and David Combes who know how to run a restaurant and bar. It's called L.P. (short for long player record) as Grant was a famous DJ. Happy hour is weekdays 5–7pm. Instagrammers be aware: after 7pm there's a ban on 'personal computing devices' at L.P.

POCKET TIP
L.P. is complemented by E.P. (short for extended play) downstairs, a restaurant offering a sensational mix of Fijian, Chinese, Indian and Thai flavours.

8 THE ROGER ROOM

370 N La Cienega Blvd
310 854 1300
Mon–Fri 6pm–2am,
Sat 7pm–2am, Sun 8pm–2am
[MAP p. 152 B3]

Fancy a no-fuss, mellow WeHo hang? Head directly to The Roger Room. The booths are comfortable and the lighting is subtle with the music set low enough that you can really talk. There's no scene, nor velvet rope outside this hidden bar where two neon tarot cards act as signage. Inside is a lushly decorated room with a nod to turn-of-the-century decadence: dark woods, deep reds and vintage murals. Cocktails rule here with the friendly bar staff in charge of a creative menu featuring classic and house concoctions. Tijuana Brass is a refreshing mix of white tequila, lime juice and cucumber foam whilst Thug's blend of bourbon, honey liqueur, lemon juice and habanero bitters certainly packs a wallop. Want to reserve a booth? They do take reservations if you call.

THE BEACHES

With an average of 300 days of sunshine, any visit to LA needs to include a sunset viewing over the Pacific with palms in the foreground. You just need to decide where to go to get the best vista: the pier at Santa Monica, the boardwalk at Venice, beachside in Malibu or at any one of the restaurants or bars that line the shore. Of course, there's so much else to do other than gazing at the sunset or swimming and surfing. The Santa Monica Pier (see p. 38) is worth a wander and abutting Santa Monica's south side is Venice Beach (see p. 38), simply called Venice to locals. Walk along the beachfront boardwalk and take in the atmosphere, you'll see entertainers, buffed men and women and skaters. Keen shoppers should head to Venice's Abbot Kinney Boulevard (see p. 42), and bike enthusiasts can take a tour with Bike Center (see p. 38) from Santa Monica to Venice Beach. If you're a design fan you must visit Eames House (see p. 40) for a key example of mid-century-modern architecture.

Further up the Pacific Coast Highway is Malibu, home to many Hollywood celebs and musicians. It's laid-back, scenic and it's surprisingly easy to find a park near the beach. Find the best break by chatting with the local surfers at Boardriders Malibu (see p. 44) or stop by Neptune's Net (see p. 46) for fresh seafood.

The Expo Metro Lines can get you from Downtown to Santa Monica, but a car is a definite plus for cruising along up to Malibu, windows down, with a California mixtape (see p. 144) playing.

→ *Paddleboarding in the Pacific by Malibu Pier*

SIGHTS
1. Bike Center Guided Tour
2. Westward Beach
3. Eames House

SHOPPING
4. Abbot Kinney Boulevard
5. Boardriders Malibu

EATING
6. Gjelina Take Away
7. Neptune's Net
8. Sidecar Doughnuts & Coffee

DRINKING
9. ONYX Rooftop Lounge

1 BIKE CENTER GUIDED TOUR

1555 2nd St, Santa Monica
310 656 8500
Mon–Sun 8am–6pm
Tours Mon–Sun 11am–2pm
[MAP p. 171 E3]

It's an easy pedal from Santa Monica to Venice Beach (around 13 kilometres/8 miles return), made all the better with commentary along the way. On this laid-back cycling tour with Bike Center you can enjoy the great outdoors along one of the world's most famous beachside promenades. See the fitness fanatics flexing at **Muscle Beach**, the carny rides at **Santa Monica Pier** and the prowess of the skaters at **Venice skatepark**. After that head towards the **Venice Boardwalk** and stop for an ice-cream at one of the colourful stores in the area. You'll also get to tour the Venice man-made **canals**, built in 1905 by developer Abbot Kinney as part of his grand plan to recreate the appearance and feel of the Italian city in California. If only the gondoliers that once plied the waters were still here.

POCKET TIP

A Camera Obscura resides at the Camera Obscura Art Lab (1450 Ocean Ave). This Victorian-era optical marvel (built in 1898) is accessible and free every day except Sunday.

2 WESTWARD BEACH

7103 Westward Beach Rd, Malibu
[MAP p. 173 B3]

Want a dip in the ocean? Forget crowded Venice or Santa Monica, head up to Malibu but be strategic. Eschew the popular main Zuma Beach (too many people) but right next door, hidden away off Pacific Coast Highway, is Westward Beach. What's more if you get there early enough there's free roadside parking, and if not, there's a giant carpark next door at Point Dume Headlands State Park that will only cost you $8 for the day. The beach is patrolled by lifeguards who sit in their *Baywatch* towers (incidentally the TV show was often filmed around here), be sure to swim between the flags, the designated safest area to swim. There's also quality restrooms with outdoor showers. Dolphins frolic near the shore and up on the cliff celebrity homes look over the bay.

POCKET TIP

Feel like some exercise after lazing on the beach? Take a hike. The southern end of Westward ends at Point Dume cliff and there are hiking trails that lead inland to Point Dume Natural Preserve.

39

3 EAME/ HOU/E

203 Chautauqua Blvd,
Pacific Palisades
310 459 9663
Mon–Tues 10am–4pm,
Thurs–Sat 10am–4pm
[MAP p. 170 C2]

If you're a mid-century-modern design fan then you need to see this house. Husband-and-wife Charles and Ray Eames were an inspirational design couple. Their home, also known as Case Study House No. 8, high on a hill in Pacific Palisades just north of Santa Monica, was designed and constructed in 1949. The couple lived there until their deaths: Charles in 1978 and Ray, ten years to the day, in 1988. Left exactly as it was, the home is full of artworks, candelabras, furniture they designed and a jungle of indoor plants. The $10 exterior tour includes a history lesson from a docent. The bonus is that with mid-century architecture the windows are floor-to-ceiling so you can peek inside; no need to pay the $275 (and up) for an interior tour. The verdant garden and views out to the ocean only add to the splendour. Bookings for exterior visits are required at least 48 hours in advance, see its website (www.eamesfoundation.org) for details.

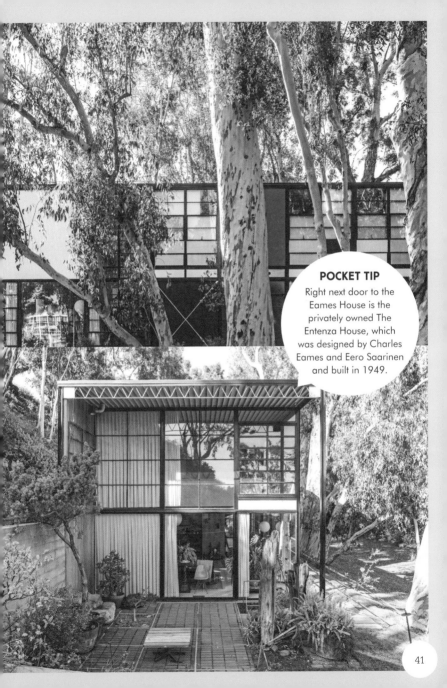

POCKET TIP
Right next door to the Eames House is the privately owned The Entenza House, which was designed by Charles Eames and Eero Saarinen and built in 1949.

4 ABBOT KINNEY BOULEVARD

Abbot Kinney Blvd, Venice
Hours vary
[MAP p. 172 B2]

This mile-long boulevard named after Abbot Kinney, the Italian-loving developer of Venice Beach has become one of LA's most popular shopping strips. Don't expect to see big name chain stores here, as it's strictly for cutting-edge creatives, whether in the food industry, fashion, design, fitness and, well, cannabis (*see* p. 143). Cannabis brand to the stars, **Dosist** recently opened their first bricks-and-mortar store here immaculately designed with limestone floors and white maple-wood walls. Other highlights include **Burro** (and **Burro Kids** next door) for cool California-centric gifts, and eyewear at **Warby Parker**. Look too for the range of street murals. It's also here on Abbot Kinney that the City of LA's first **rainbow crosswalk** is, in recognition of the 50th anniversary of the Stonewall Uprising.

POCKET TIP

If you happen to be in town, Abbot Kinney First Fridays (every first Friday of the month) brings the party out into the street with food trucks and music.

5 BOARDRIDER/ MALIBU

18820 CA-1, Malibu
310 359 8274
Mon–Sun 10am–7pm
[MAP p. 146 B3]

As you drive up the Pacific Coast Highway you can't miss the architecturally designed Boardriders Malibu showroom; it sits above a perfect point break on a picturesque stretch of cliff overlooking Topanga Beach. Modelled on former Quicksilver CEO Pierre Agnes' original French Boardriders store, this is not just a place to buy surf gear. Although they do stock a big range of boards, clothing and accessories, it is as much a place for surfers to hang out, get some tips on the best breaks, a haircut at the in-store **barber shop** or just chill on the terrace and take in the sweeping ocean views. The staff (all local surfers) is friendly and knowledgeable and Boardriders regularly host surf film screenings, art events, yoga classes, signings, free gigs, food trucks and product launches. Check its social media for details.

6 GJELINA TAKE AWAY

1427 Abbot Kinney Blvd, Venice
310 392 7575
Mon–Sun 7am–10pm
[MAP p. 172 C2]

Want simply prepared seasonal food served in a flash? Come here. We're talking menus of sandwiches (try the poached tuna melt), oven-baked pizzas and fancy salads, the latter so fresh it feels like the dirt has just been washed off those kale leaves. It's the take-away outpost of perennially popular Gjelina restaurant next door and for those that want a cheaper, quicker option. There's a small amount of seating in the wood-panelled room and one outdoor bench. It's not a place to linger but the memory of that crunchy bread (baked onsite) sandwich or salad will have you returning again before your trip is through. Or you can take more than the memories with you and buy the cookbook.

POCKET TIP

Venice Beach Boardwalk is famous for its shops and restaurants and legendary for buskers. You'll see anything from old-school hip hop to a guitar playing heavy metal 'robot' on rollerskates.

45

7 NEPTUNE'S NET

42505 Pacific Coast Hwy,
Malibu
310 457 3095
Mon–Thurs 10.30am–8pm,
Fri 10.30am–9pm, Sat–Sun
10am–8.30pm, winter
hours vary
[MAP p. 172 C2]

The drive up Pacific Coast Highway is beautiful (ocean on the left, mansions on the right) and the reward of having a meal at Neptune's Net makes it even more tantalising. Neptune's Net is by no means fancy but with its inexpensive seafood, people-watching, including some of Malibu's longest standing old salts, and film fame, it's worth stopping by; you may recognise it for its appearance in *Point Break* and *The Fast and the Furious*. Choose from the battered type of seafood in one room and fresh in the other. It's a hearty meal, the seafood comes with corn on the cobb, a side of vegetables and bread. Leave room for their New England clam chowder, which can be served in a sourdough bread bowl. Outdoor seats are hard to come by, but if you're here during the week you're likely to snag one (or indoors). Beware – the portaloos out the back are not ideal.

8 SIDECAR DOUGHNUTS & COFFEE

631 Wilshire Blvd, Santa Monica
310 587 0022
Sun–Thurs 6.30am–6pm,
Fri–Sat 6.30am–9pm
[MAP p. 171 E2]

Most LA doughnut shops are pretty run of the mill – the usual glazed variety – but Sidecar really stands out. Why? One word ... huckleberry. All doughnuts are made onsite and this one, its trademark, involves springy cake dough flecked with huckleberries. The berry glaze is bright pink and incredibly scrumptious. If huckleberry doesn't sound like your thing, there are a variety of flavours on any given day and the beauty is the team keep baking, so each batch is fresh from the oven. They also occasionally offer a 'chef series', which involves collaborations with some of LA's top chefs to create limited-edition decadent delights. There's a weekly gluten-free option on the menu, too. Oh, and they do a decent coffee – they have their own signature blend.

POCKET TIP
To see what the blowout bar (hair blow-drying) craze is all about, try a 15-minute express at Glam+Go in the Fairmont Miramar Hotel & Bungalows (101 Wilshire Blvd, Santa Monica).

47

9 ONYX ROOFTOP LOUNGE

Shangri-La Hotel, 1301 Ocean
Ave, Santa Monica
310 394 2791
Mon–Wed 4pm–12am,
Thurs 4pm–2am, Fri–Sat
3pm–2am, Sun 3pm–12am
[MAP p. 171 D3]

At the end of a long day of
exercising, shopping or eating,
there's nothing better than
to down a frosty brew from a
rooftop with a view, namely
an ocean view. One of the
best vistas on the West Coast
is at ONYX on the rooftop of
the Shangri-La Hotel in Santa
Monica. The design is a mix
of Rat Pack, Studio 54 and
space age, which suits the
soundtrack – a mix of disco,
glam rock and beats – but the
view is pure California, with
the Pacific Ocean and endless
palm trees framing the sunset.
Cocktails here are named after
famous songs, with London
Calling featuring British gin
and fresh botanicals and
Purple Haze given its hue by
adding lavender to gin. The
Shangri-La, built in 1939 in Art
Deco-style, started as a beach
getaway for film stars.

POCKET TIP

It's California so every cool vantage point relates to the silver screen. The Shangri-La was the filming location for the *The Assassination of Gianni Versace*, as it resembles the style of South Beach in Miami, where Gianni Versace lived and was murdered.

BEVERLY HILLS & CULVER CITY

Long the domain of LA's old money, the westside of Los Angeles, that is Beverly Hills and closer toward the ocean, Culver City and surrounds, is the place to go to see some of the city's more leafy districts. Think gated mansions, wide avenues and sightseeing buses winding up the boulevards toward the mountains. This area has for a century been the 'home to the stars'. It began with the Pickfair estate, the famous abode built for Douglas Fairbanks and Mary Pickford in 1919, and soon others like Will Rogers and Rudolph Valentino followed. Of course, the most well-known street is Rodeo Drive, the very mention of which conjures up thoughts of luxury shopping and fancy cars. It's worth a look, just to see the spectacle and to visit The Beverly Wilshire (see p. 52), but there are other areas on the westside that are equally interesting, including the back streets of Culver City where warehouses have been converted into coffee roasters and a new shopping and lifestyle precinct (Platform, see p. 56) has recently opened.

There's galleries and museums to explore in this precinct, and do make sure you visit The Museum of Jurassic Technology (see p. 54), as it almost defies explanation. Old-school eateries prevail such as Nate 'n Al Delicatessen (see p. 57) and The Apple Pan (see p. 58), as do newer, upscale choices, though the latter tend to be on the pricey side.

Now to the thorny issue of transport. You can take the Expo Metro Line to Culver City from Santa Monica but you really need wheels to get to Beverly Hills. Until the Metro Purple line expands that way there's always the bus or Uber/Lyft.

↠ *Window shopping on Rodeo Drive, Beverly Hills*

SIGHTS
1. The Beverly Wilshire
2. Hammer Museum
3. The Museum of Jurassic Technology

SHOPPING
4. andSons Chocolatiers
5. Platform

EATING
6. Nate 'n Al Delicatessen
7. The Apple Pan

DRINKING
8. Bar Nine

1 THE BEVERLY WILSHIRE

9500 Wilshire Blvd, Beverly Hills
310 275 5200
Mon–Sun 6.30am–10.30pm
[MAP p. 159 E3]

You'll want to walk down Rodeo Drive just to see the spectacle of high-end retail, and even if you're not much of a shopper, the front bar called **The Blvd** of The Beverly Wilshire is the place to settle down for a champagne after any expedition to 90210. Not only is this where *Pretty Woman* was set, Elvis also once lived here when he was filming during the 1960s. The Beverly Wilshire offers a small peek into how the super-rich live and there's a wealth of star-spotting opportunities. On my recent visit, Christopher Plummer was meeting with a friend for a drink; proper Hollywood royalty right there. Want to really ramp up the indulgence factor? Their 'Pretty Woman for a Day' experience gets you behind-the-scenes at some of Rodeo Drive's most famous fashion houses.

POCKET TIP
Rodeo Drive is a top destination for celebrity spotting and window shopping. On weekends there's a free trolley service (a bus which resembles a cable car) between 11am and 5pm that runs from the Civic Center and stops at Rodeo Drive.

2 HAMMER MUSEUM

10899 Wilshire Blvd
310 443 7000
Tues–Fri 11am–8pm,
Sat–Sun 11am–5pm
[MAP p. 158 A4]

There is a lot of art to view in Los Angeles, so what makes the Hammer Museum worth the trip? At Hammer, exhibitions change frequently and it's not just a matter of viewing art, you get the real interaction; there are regular screenings, talks, workshops, forums and poetry readings across the three floors. The impressive collection of European and American paintings and drawings reflects the interests and passion of the museum's founder, Armand Hammer. The permanent collection includes work by Monet, Gauguin, Van Gogh and Toulouse-Lautrec. Entry to the museum is free due to generous donors, including from the late Leonard Nimoy (aka Spock). There's ample parking directly below the museum.

POCKET TIP

Also worth checking out is the onsite restaurant, Audrey. It's gone viral on Instagram since opening. Think velvet booths in blush and olive, elaborate chandeliers and tiled walls by artist Jorge Pardo.

3 THE MUSEUM OF JURASSIC TECHNOLOGY

9341 Venice Blvd, Culver City
310 836 6131
Thurs 2pm–8pm,
Fri–Sun 12pm–6pm
[MAP p. 161 D3]

'What is this place?' you might wonder as you wander the darkened halls of The Museum of Jurassic Technology. It's a collection of cultural curiosities housed in a huge museum hidden behind an unremarkable doorway. The museum says its mandate is to lead you from familiar objects to the unfamiliar and this selection of oddities from the (seemingly mythical) 'Lower Jurassic' does just that. The atmosphere is solemn, staff are polite but distant and low-lit cases display forgotten technologies, strange folk art and curious artefacts. It's a reality altering place that defies definition, but if you're prepared to take on the mystery and confusion it's an enjoyable experience that is both strangely calming and confounding. As we ascended the stairs to take tea and biscuits in the rooftop garden aviary we were still quietly asking the question, 'What is this place?' Entrance is $8 and well worth it.

POCKET TIP

LA's oddest zoo is Star Eco Station (10101 Jefferson Blvd, Culver City), a rescue home for exotic pets that doubles as a wildlife sanctuary. They care for everything from parrots and peacocks to crocodiles and tigers.

4 ANDSONS CHOCOLATIERS

9548 Brighton Way, Beverly Hills
310 276 2776
Mon–Sat 10am–6pm,
Sun 11am–5pm
[MAP p.159 E3]

If you love chocolate, this
is the store to put on your
list. Eschew Beverly Hills
chocolate stalwarts, Teuscher,
and head across the road
to andSons. What makes
andSons standout? Owners,
Marc and Phil Covitz work
with chocolatier Kriss Harvey,
formerly of the Bazaar by José
Andres, to create modern
flavours such as tart yuzu and
lime and passionfruit caramel
made with milk chocolate.
Colourful bonbons, truffles,
chocolate nuts, caramels and
bars are made using produce
from local farmers' markets.
The space, complete with a
small cafe, was designed by
celebrity interior designer,
Nate Berkus and features
a mural of cacao pods that
snakes across the ceiling. It's
impossible to leave without a
box of delicious treats.

5 PLATFORM

8850 Washington Blvd,
Culver City
Mon–Sun 7am–10pm
[MAP p. 161 E2]

The Southern California climate lends itself well to outdoor malls filled with tables, chairs, benches and umbrellas but Platform goes a step further with captivating murals including Jen Stark's *Technicolor Drip* on display and verdant greenery. Here you can browse British designer **Tom Dixon**, **Poketo** (*see* p. 66), **Import News** with a great selection of international zines and **Aesop** skincare, as well as fashion boutiques and pop-up stores. Sign up to its website (www.platformla.com) for news and upcoming sales. There's a **SoulCycle** spin class studio here too (their largest in LA), should you be so inclined to get involved. Retail outlets take over the ground floor with offices up above. Finish the shopping expedition off with a rooftop drink at **Margot**, where panoramic views are on offer from the patio. Another plus? It's right across the Metro Expo Line station, and there's free wi-fi.

POCKET TIP

Enigmatic superstar Tim Robbins still runs the Actors' Gang (9070 Venice Blvd, Culver City), a theatre company he founded in the '80s. They stage edgy and experimental productions in a former electrical substation.

6 NATE 'N AL DELICATESSEN

414 N Beverly Dr, Beverly Hills
310 274 0101
Mon–Sun 7am–9pm
[MAP p. 159 E3]

Los Angeles has a lot of great neighbourhood Jewish deli/diners, and these places are usually packed with character (and characters). But Nate 'n Al's is a definite standout. For the last 70 years it has been serving the kind of diner comfort food that's easy to crave. On a recent visit, we lined up just as the lunchtime crowd was starting to build and the maître-d' was kind and patient dealing with the customers on a gentle first-name basis. You get the feeling that it's a social dance that happens every day. We were soon seated drinking mugs of excellent black coffee and munching on dill pickles. The matzoh ball soup is a gentle cloud of savoury dumpling sitting in a simple broth. The hot pastrami sandwich is bang on too; delicate slow-cooked meat piled on slices of crusty double-baked rye with some slaw on the side. It's one of those perfect lunchtime meals.

POCKET TIP

Get your nails treated like a Hollywood celebrity at an affordable price at Olive & June (430 N Canon Dve, Beverly Hills). This salon offers luxury and personalised service with 35 colours, including organic polishes.

57

7 THE APPLE PAN

10801 Pico Blvd
310 475 3585
Sun–Thurs 11am–12am, Fri–Sat
11am–1am
[MAP p. 160 A1]

Some places in LA never change and are all the better for that fact. The Apple Pan is exactly one of these places and to go there is to understand you're stepping back in time. A supremely authentic burger joint that's been serving the same cooked-to-order flame-grilled burgers, superb hand-cut fries, sandwiches and fresh baked pies since 1947. The counter service is gruff but pleasant and you'll watch ravenously as your food is cooked in the open kitchen the same way they've been doing it for 70 years. The Hickory burger is the go-to here, a smoky delight on a fresh bun, simple yet perfect. It's a timeless dish (accompanied by those crisp, faultless fries) that is worth travelling to experience. The decor is timeless too, with walls papered in red plaid and red leather stools positioned around a wood-panelled counter. By the way, it's cash only (be sure to check out the vintage cash registers) but rest easy, there's a bank with cash machines right next door.

8 BAR NINE

3515 Helms Ave, Culver City
310 837 7815
Mon–Sun 8am–5pm
[MAP p. 161 E3]

Follow the aroma of coffee to a
spacious warehouse in a back
street of Culver City to discover
Bar Nine, where you'll see a
giant Probat roaster taking
pride of place in the room.
Bar Nine roast twice a week,
producing a range of bright
and fruity blends. It's a good
place to hang, with friendly
staff and Angelenos on laptops
enjoying their cold brews and
espressos. The long wooden
coffee bar and industrial feel
works well in the space. They
also run classes on how to
pour latte art (you know, those
love heart presentations in
the crema) and how to brew
espresso, so you can take the
experience home with you.

59

DOWNTOWN

Who says you can't walk in LA or cycle for that matter? Welcome to Downtown LA, where amongst freshly planted trees and newly deposited street furniture, skateboarders weave and pedestrians joyfully wander. No need for a hire car when you're planning a stay here, everything is within hoofing distance. Besides, if you were driving you might miss the street art from a Banksy on South Broadway to a giant mural bigger than a football field towering above the Pershing Square Metro station. Plus, Chinatown on the north-east of Downtown is a definite must-visit, with an array of great restaurants such as Howlin' Ray's (see p. 70).

Once full of flophouses (cheap motels) and sprawling carparks, in the last decade Downtown LA has been transformed. It's home to some of modern art's greatest hits (Warhol! Lichtenstein! Koons!) at The Broad (see p. 62), as well as other cultural institution giants, including one of the world's best libraries, the Los Angeles Public Library (see p. 63). There's also cool venues and bars, including the Imperial Western Beer Company (see p. 72) in Union Station and Clifton's (see p. 73). Indeed, once derelict buildings are being revived. Hip new boutiques, barista joints and restaurants are popping up weekly. Think LA is one big spread out urban sprawl with no centre? You need to visit Downtown, it's one of the city's most exciting precincts to be right now.

You can easily hire a Metro Bike to get around Downtown for as little as $5 a day. There are numerous bike stations in the precinct, all you need to do is download the Metro Bike Share App to unlock.

→ Union Station is worth visiting for the architecture

SIGHTS
1. The Broad
2. Los Angeles Public Library
3. Olvera Street

SHOPPING
4. The Last Bookstore
5. Poketo Project Space @ Row DTLA

SHOPPING & EATING
6. Grand Central Market
7. Mercado La Paloma

EATING
8. Howlin' Ray's
9. Philippe

DRINKING
10. Imperial Western Beer Company
11. Clifton's

1 THE BROAD

221 S Grand Ave
213 232 6200
Tues–Wed 11am–5pm,
Thurs–Fri 11am–8pm,
Sat 10am–8pm,
Sun 10am–6pm
[MAP p.148 B2]

Skip the queues and reserve an advance free ticket to the Broad Museum via its website (www.thebroad.org). This is one museum that's popular with both selfie-loving social media influencers and art lovers. Founded by philanthropists Eli and Edythe Broad, the museum's permanent collection gallery includes a 2000-piece collection of contemporary art, featuring works by the likes of Andy Warhol (including *Single Elvis*), Cindy Sherman and Roy Lichtenstein. Some say the building itself overshadows the impressive collection of modern art. Designed by architectural firm Diller Scofidio + Renfro, in collaboration with Gensler, in 2015, the design merges the two key components of the building: public exhibition space and collection storage otherwise known as the 'vault' – the Broad's extensive lending library. Take a peek – you can see it through the glass as you take the escalator to the second level.

POCKET TIP

Just across from The Broad is the main branch of The Museum of Contemporary Art (MOCA). If you don't want to fork out the $15 entry fee, save the visit for Thursday when it's free to visit from 5–8pm.

2 LOS ANGELES PUBLIC LIBRARY

630 W 5th St
213 228 7000
Mon–Thurs 10am–8pm,
Fri–Sat 9.30am–5.30pm,
Sun 1pm–5pm
[MAP p.148 A3]

This isn't any library. Just walk into the eight-storey atrium and look up at the chandelier that represents the solar system, with the globe surrounded by planets, and you'll see it's something more. Take the elevators and you'll see an art installation lining the walls featuring old catalogue cards with book titles beginning with 'complete' or 'comprehensive'. Housing more than two million books, the Central Library's Rare Books Department alone has over 16,000 volumes, dating from the 15th century, and a collection of over three million historic photographs. There's also regular free author events here, check the website (www.lapl.org) for details. Take one of the daily docent-led tours of the historic library where you can learn about the 1926 Bertram Goodhue Building and visit its rooftops gardens full of fountains and sculptures, as well as learn about the disastrous 1986 fire.

3 OLVERA STREET

845 N Alameda St
Mon–Fri 10am–7pm,
Sat–Sun 10am–10pm
[MAP p.149 D2]

Celebrating the city's Mexican culture and heritage, Olvera Street is an outdoor brick-paved pedestrian plaza flanked by Mexican folk art stores, restaurants and the pleasing sounds of wandering mariachi musicians. Free events are often held here including the annual Blessing of the Animals (in March or April), which involves a celebratory procession of humans and pets. Be sure to walk around the oldest house in Los Angeles, **Avila Adobe** from 1818 at 10 Olvera Street. The house is furnished as a typical ranchero would have looked in the 1840s with Spanish colonial-style furniture. A central courtyard features a cactus garden. It's free to tour. Olvera Street is across the road from Union Station.

POCKET TIP
It's impossible to leave Olvera Street without trying fresh hot churros from Mr Churro, the aroma permeates the air.

4 THE LAST BOOKSTORE

453 S Spring St
213 488 0599
Sun–Thurs 10am–10pm,
Fri–Sat 10am–11pm
[MAP p. 148 B3]

It might not actually be the last bookstore but it might be the final one you need to visit; this is definitely one of the biggest and best in town. The Last Bookstore stocks more than 250,000 new and used books across a huge space with a catalogue that pretty much covers every genre imaginable. A large and reasonably priced selection of used vinyl will keep music nerds busy for hours and the new **Arts & Rare Book Annex** contains dozens of rare titles, cool posters and art pieces. Originally opened as an online store in a small, Downtown loft in 2005, the store moved to its current location (a former bank) in 2011 as the project to revitalise Downtown gained momentum. The Last Bookstore also hosts book signings, discussion panels and a range of book clubs for everything from horror novels to LGBTIQ+ authors.

5 POKETO PROJECT SPACE @ ROW DTLA

777 S Alameda St #174
213 372 5686
Mon–Sun 11am–5pm
[MAP p. 147 E3]

Fostering an appreciation of graphic design and the work of makers and artists, husband-and-wife team Ted Vadakan and Angie Myung came up with the concept of Poketo, a carefully curated collection of design-conscious goods. We're talking well-designed small knick-knacks that are useful and easy to bring home, like phone cases, stationery, totes and caps. The beauty of this is that it's a concept space where there are pop-ups showing off the work of different brands, artists, designers and makers. There are also regular workshops so depending on when you visit, you can book in for wall art workshops, as well as paper flower making, painting with natural dyes and braided rug weaving. Buy something artisan-made and unleash your own creativity while you're here.

POCKET TIP
There's also a Poketo at Platform LA (see p. 56) and another at The Line Hotel in Koreatown.

6 GRAND CENTRAL MARKET

317 S Broadway
Mon–Sun 8am–10pm
[MAP p.148 B3]

Since 1917 this Downtown landmark has been offering the budget-conscious connoisseur a world-spanning smorgasbord of places to eat. Grand Central Market is perfectly placed as a meal stop during a Downtown sojourn. There's a whole bunch of Downtown landmarks right nearby and the market is now open until 10pm every night. But what to eat? Ever popular newcomers like **Eggslut**, **Bell Campo Meat Company** and **Wexler's Deli** add a hipness quotient but for a real taste of old-school Downtown LA, it's hard to go past **Roast To Go**, an antojito joint serving excellent Mexican street food since 1952. For something different, **Saritas** does great pupusas (El Salvadorean corn cakes) and was featured in the movie *La La Land*. Round off your meal with a couple of scoops from **McConnell's Fine Ice Cream**.

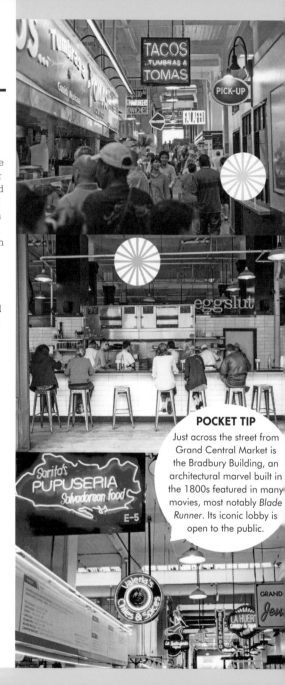

POCKET TIP

Just across the street from Grand Central Market is the Bradbury Building, an architectural marvel built in the 1800s featured in many movies, most notably *Blade Runner*. Its iconic lobby is open to the public.

POCKET TIP

Angel's Flight has been a Downtown icon since 1901. This two car incline railroad that runs up Bunker Hill is known as the 'world's shortest railroad'.

7 MERCADO LA PALOMA

3655 S Grand Ave
213 748 1963
Sun–Tues 8am–9pm,
Wed–Thurs 7am–9pm,
Fri–Sat 8am–10pm
[MAP p. 154 C4]

Housed in a former textile factory just south of Downtown, Mercado La Paloma is not only a great place to eat but also serves as a centre for the local community, providing medical services, meeting spaces and other essentials. The upshot is that when you come here to eat or shop, you are helping a community that's long been ignored by wider Los Angeles. But what should you eat? Folks flock from all over town to dine at **Chichen Itza**, Yucatan cuisine with superb takes on classics like cochinita pibil and pollo asado. **Holbox** is a killer seafood stand where the ceviche and fish tacos are the stuff of legend. There's also great Ethiopian and Thai food, along with an excellent burger stand. If you're looking for mementos, there's Oaxacan folk art to buy and Yucatan artisanal products.

8 HOWLIN' RAY'S

Far East Plaza 727 N Broadway
#128
213 935 8399
Tues–Fri 11am–7pm,
Sat–Sun 10am–7pm
[MAP p. 149 D1]

Nashville Hot Chicken (fried chicken liberally dusted with a hot spice mix) is hugely popular and some of LA's best is in Chinatown at Howlin' Ray's. There's a catch however, Howlin' Ray's is so insanely popular that you can expect to queue for at least a couple of hours. On a recent visit, we arrived at 10.30am and the line was already long, and by the time Ray's tiny storefront opened it was snaking around the corner. There was a cult-like atmosphere in the queue, behind us a couple of fellas from Fresno were making their monthly pilgrimage and the mood was surprisingly upbeat, it was obvious a lot of these folks had done this before. Is it worth the wait? Well, if you like fried chicken it is; a good quality organic bird and crispy buttermilk batter at varying levels of heat from mild to Howlin' make this a great meal for the very patient.

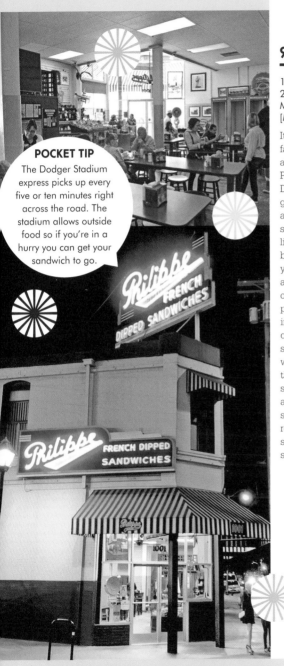

POCKET TIP

The Dodger Stadium express picks up every five or ten minutes right across the road. The stadium allows outside food so if you're in a hurry you can get your sandwich to go.

9 PHILIPPE

1001 N Alameda St
213 628 3781
Mon–Sun 6am–10pm
[MAP p. 149 D1]

It's a tradition for baseball fans to start game days with a French Dip Sandwich from Philippe before heading to Dodger Stadium. This custom goes back almost a century and with good reason: these sandwiches are excellent. A light crusty roll is dipped in beef jus and then filled with your choice of meat and cheese and accompanied by sides of crunchy dill pickles, bright purple boiled eggs pickled in beet juice and excellent coleslaw. There's a quality selection of beer on tap as well and in one corner even the original 1920s concession stand selling gum, newspapers and candy. Philippe's sawdust-strewn dining room hasn't really changed in decades, so you'll really feel like you're stepping back in time.

10 IMPERIAL WE/TERN BEER COMPANY

800 N Alameda St
213 270 0035
Mon–Thurs 3pm–12am,
Fri 3pm–2am, Sat 12pm–2am,
Sun 12pm–12am
[MAP p. 149 E2]

There are regular brewpubs, and there are brewpubs that even the non-drinker will love. This is the latter. Housed at Union Station and unused for 50 years, celebrated Downtown restaurateurs Cedd Moses and Eric Needleman have done an incredible job bringing the Art Deco grandeur back into this giant room; they worked with the L.A. Conservancy to restore historical features and tile work. Imperial Western also houses a 15-barrel brewery and you can sample all its craft beers from the bar taps. Come here in the late afternoon and see the sunlight stream in, highlighting the intricately restored soaring ceiling. There's pool, shuffleboard and checkers to play and bar snacks to sate any hunger.

POCKET TIP
Next door is The Streamliner, done out like a Streamline Moderne train carriage. It's dark and moody, and has more of a late-night vibe, perfect for a gimlet before heading on that last train out of town.

11 CLIFTON'S

648 S Broadway
213 627 1673
Thurs–Sat 6pm–2am
[MAP p. 148 B4]

A Downtown institution since 1935, the recent reopening of Clifton's saw lines snake down Broadway, with thousands eager to check out the new look. The original owner, Clifford Clinton had a policy to never turn anyone away, whether they could pay for their hot meal or not, and once served up to 15,000 patrons a day. Lovingly restored with a woodsy feel – there's a giant faux redwood, a waterfall and taxidermied beasts eyeing you off over the five floors, Clifton's is now known mostly for its array of bars. Writer Ray Bradbury spent decades holding court at Clifton's and there's still a corner booth dedicated to him, and Jack Kerouac wrote about it in *On the Road*. Don't be surprised if you see David Lynch drinking a mocktail in the Monarch Bar, he's a fan.

POCKET TIP

In Sheep's Clothing is a Tokyo-styled 'Hi-Fi Bar'. The bartender pours drinks whilst curating a vinyl-only playlist on a system worth hundreds of thousands of dollars. Two rules: keep the talking down and no requests!

MIDTOWN

Encompassing Fairfax, La Brea and mid-Wilshire down to Koreatown, or K-town to locals, this area is one of the most densely packed parts of Los Angeles. Shooting west of Downtown, Wilshire Boulevard is the artery road and at its heart is what's known as The Miracle Mile between La Brea and Fairfax. In 1921, this stretch of Wilshire Boulevard was just a dirt road, flanked by barley fields and oil wells. In the 1930s it became a hub for department stores housed in elaborate Art Deco buildings.

Today, the strip is the place to go for culture with the Los Angeles County Museum of Art (LACMA, *see* p. 78), as well as the La Brea Tar Pits (*see* p. 77) with still-bubbling pools of real tar. Closer to Downtown, Asian restaurants and Korean spas abound in K-town. Head here when you're in need of relaxation – Beverly Hot Springs (*see* p. 80) is a great choice – and great (inexpensive) food, including A-Won Restaurant (*see* p. 82). Korean immigrants began populating Koreatown in the 1930s, with another influx in the 1960s, and the official title was designated in 1980. Art Deco buildings dot Wilshire all the way to Downtown, a few housing historic theatres where you can see some of the biggest bands in the business. Don't just look at the stage, admire the starburst ceilings and intricate tiles of the building at the El Rey Theatre (*see* p. 76).

Koreatown can be accessed by the Metro Purple Line and it's currently under construction to travel further west (encompassing The Miracle Mile).

→ *The skyline is changing along Wilshire Boulevard*

SIGHTS
1. El Rey Theatre
2. La Brea Tar Pits
3. Los Angeles County Museum of Art (LACMA)
4. Beverly Hot Springs

SHOPPING & EATING
5. Original Farmers' Market

EATING
6. A-Won Restaurant
7. Dino's Chicken and Burgers

EATING & DRINKING
8. Here's Looking At You

1 EL REY THEATRE

5515 Wilshire Blvd
323 936 6400
Opening times vary, check
website
[MAP p. 147 D3]

Built in 1936 as a movie house, the El Rey has been hosting an eclectic array of music since the early '90s. This iconic Midtown theatre is one of the best spots to see concerts in the city – from emerging artists to old-school legacy acts. The room is large, larger than its 770 capacity would suggest, meaning that it never gets overcrowded and for those lucky enough, there's a VIP mezzanine with its own bar. It's a well-run venue; even at a sold-out show it is quick and easy to grab a beverage. The sound system is state of the art and security is handled expertly and without too much fuss. Toilet attendants are there to offer towels and other amenities, so if you need to spend a penny it's best to make sure you've got a few dollar bills in your pocket. Check the website (www.theelrey.com) for shows and book ahead.

GOLDENVOICE PRESENTS
LEE FIELDS
JUNE 7

POCKET TIP

The 14 screen Pacific Theatre at The Grove is popular amongst moviegoers. If you prefer outdoor movies, in summer The Grove hosts drive-in movies on top of its multi-level carpark.

POCKET TIP

There's plenty for motorheads to do at the Petersen Automotive Museum (6060 Wilshire Blvd). The highlight? The Forza Motorsport Racing Experience, a state-of-the-art driving simulator, included in the entry fee.

2 LA BREA TAR PIT/

5801 Wilshire Blvd
323 934 7243
Mon–Sun 9.30am–5pm
[MAP p. 153 C4]

Part museum and part working palaeontological dig, LA's famous La Brea tar pits have a history that extends back over 50,000 years when mammoths, sabretooth tigers and other megafauna roamed during the Ice Age, some becoming trapped and then encased in the sticky asphalt tar of the pit. In the early part of the 20th century, the scientific importance of the site was recognised and ever since it has given up an incredible treasure-trove of Ice Age fossils. The tar pits centre is comprised of the free-to-enter **Hancock Park** that contains a green space studded by the pitch-black lakes of bubbling asphalt, you can smell the sulphur in the air. Luckily the over-curious can't get too close, as it's fenced off. The **museum** itself is a state-of-the-art affair with interactive exhibits and an incredible array of fossils; the **Fossil Lab** is surrounded by glass so you can watch as scientists uncover even more secrets of the pit.

3 LOƧ ANGELEƧ COUNTY MUƧEUM OF ART (LACMA)

5905 Wilshire Blvd
323 857 6000
Mon–Tues 11am–5pm,
Thurs 11am–5pm,
Fri 11am–8pm,
Sat–Sun 10am–7pm
[MAP p. 153 B4]

Angelenos will tell you about the long-held debate on the new structure (Too expensive! Too small!) that has been years in the works, but for the visitor the four buildings that house some of the world's best artworks across centuries are perfectly fine as they are. Start your day here with a wander through the 202 streetlamps from the 1920s and '30s called *Urban Light*, an installation by the late Chris Burden that has welcomed LACMA visitors since 2008. Then make your way to see Alexander Calder's *Three Quintains* outdoor steel fountain sculpture. There's *La Gerbe* by Matisse to view, and at varying times Lichtenstein, Cezanne and Frank Stella. Time your visit for the second Tuesday of the month when it's free for all. And enhance your experience by downloading the free app for commentary (there's free wi-fi, too).

POCKET TIP

Next door to LACMA, the new Academy Museum of Motion Pictures (6067 Wilshire Blvd) by architect Renzo Piano is set to open in 2020.

4 BEVERLY HOT SPRINGS

308 N Oxford Ave
323 734 7000
Mon–Sun 9am–9pm
[MAP p. 156 A4]

POCKET TIP
The Korean American Museum, celebrating the Korean–American experience is set to open in the area in 2022.

All that driving on the highways can be a pain in the neck. Literally. Something's got to give. Why not make a day of it and soothe away any aches and pains at one of the Korean bathhouses in Koreatown? Beverly Hot Springs is up there as one of the best. Why? It's LA's only natural hot spring spa, where the thermal springs gush from a natural artesian well below. Pay $35 to spend a whole day here enjoying the use of the hot and cold pools, dry sauna and eucalyptus steam room. Nudity is required and silence is enforced (no phones). Combine with a massage treatment, where you will be scrubbed and pummelled for full soothing effect. As with any service treatment in the US, a gratuity is expected (around 20% of the treatment price).

5 ORIGINAL FARMER/ MARKET

6333 W 3rd St
323 933 9211
Mon–Fri 9am–9pm,
Sat 9am–8pm, Sun 10am–7pm
[MAP p. 153 A1]

In these days when organic farmers' markets are held in nearly every district, the name can be confusing. Yes, this is a permanent farmers' market, but it offers something more. There is great produce here, including a couple of excellent old-school butchers, poultry and seafood purveyors, plus organic fruit and veg, but this Los Angeles perennial, established in 1934, has a whole lot more going for it. There's an established selection of much loved restaurants, such as **The Gumbo Pot**, which has long been a popular spot for Louisiana favourites; and many consider **Singapore's Banana Leaf** to be one of the best hawker-style restaurants in the city. Then there's veterans like **Dupar's Pies & Diner** and **Bob's Coffee & Doughnuts** that are almost as old as the market itself. Round out your afternoon with some retail therapy, with unique shops like **Light My Fire** that sell an eye-watering range of hot sauces and **Kip's Toyland**, a delightful nostalgic toy store.

81

6 A-WON RESTAURANT

913 S Vermont Ave
213 389 6764
Mon–Sat 11am–10pm,
Sun 12.30pm–9pm
[MAP p.154 B2]

One thing about LA is that hidden amongst its thousands of strip malls are culinary gems that you would never find without the aid of word of mouth. A friend hipped me to A-Won, an unassuming Korean/Japanese eatery in Midtown that offers a range of fresh sushi, killer kimchi, Korean-style noodles, plus Japanese and Korean entrees and mains. It's an old-school LA restaurant experience with $2 valet parking and wood-lined decor. And it's fresh! While I was surverying the menu a chef walked in carrying a bucket of freshly caught fish destined for the sushi station. As the lunchtime crowd starts to build you can tell this place is popular with the locals. I recommend that you order the lunch specials, which are served bento-style with a range of accompaniments. The barbecued pork short ribs are tender and delicious, the sushi is first rate and oh man, that kimchi!

POCKET TIP
If you're poking around Koreatown and need a feed and some retail therapy, check out the historic Chapman Market. There's Japanese cosmetics at Shibuyala and a range of Korean dining options.

7 DINO'S CHICKEN AND BURGERS

2575 W Pico Blvd
213 380 3554
Mon–Thurs 6am–11pm,
Fri–Sat 6am–12am,
Sun 7am–11pm
[MAP p. 154 B2]

LA gastronomes rarely agree on much but one fact will get them all nodding: Dino's Famous Chicken is hands-down one of the best cheap meals in the city. The charcoal-grilled chicken is slathered in a spicy, luminous red sauce and served on a bed of fries (also soaked in sauce) accompanied by tortillas and a small tub of coleslaw. It's a perfect Angeleno confluence of Greek, Mexican and American food and at $7.95, it's a steal. The menu lists burgers and other diner food but everyone (and yes, be prepared to queue) seems to have their eyes on one thing – the chicken. For good reason, too, as this sloppy mess of fries, sauce and perfectly grilled chicken is delicious with just the right amount of heat. And those tortillas? Well you'll be wanting them to mop up that incandescent sauce, it's too good. The decor here is nothing fancy – it's a fast-food joint. If you can nab a table, sit outside and watch those patiently waiting smile once they hit the front of the line.

8 HERE'S LOOKING AT YOU

3901 W 6th St
213 568 3573
Sun–Thurs 6–10pm,
Fri 6–11pm, Sat 10.30am–
2.30pm & 6–11pm,
Sun 10.30am–2.30pm
[MAP p.154 A1]

POCKET TIP

Want to catch the up-and-coming talent in the sketch comedy world? Check out The Groundlings (7307 Melrose Ave), an improv theatre and school. Their alumni include Will Ferrell, Lisa Kudrow and Conan O'Brien.

Sometimes cocktails aren't just about the ingredients – they come with a story. At Here's Looking At You (the famous quote from *Casablanca*), the cocktails are designed by the season with a narrative based on some of their favourite LA-based books. For example, Evergreen, a cocktail featuring lemon verbena tea-infused tequila blanco, dimmi, tarragon-parsley syrup and lime pays homage to Evelyn Waugh finding refuge at Forest Lawn in *The Loved One*. The inventive menu adds a layer to the experience, and sampling a few, I can vouch they taste every bit as remarkable as the books they portray. The food here is incredible, too. Chef/partner Jonathan Whitener dishes up carefully crafted Californian cuisine, a highlight being the lamb shoulder chop, miso, chicory, minari, onion, togarashi. Plus, the setting is a delight, this 50-seater room has a mid-century modern design vibe with gorgeous pendant lighting and rich wooden textures.

HIGHLAND PARK & EAGLE ROCK

Right now, nowhere in Los Angeles is hipper than Highland Park and Eagle Rock in the city's north-east. With real estate prices heading into the domain of squillionaires in Silver Lake and Los Feliz, more creative types are heading to this precinct to set up homes (Craftsman homes are big here), as well as shops, bars and restaurants. What was once up-and-coming has now definitely arrived. Want to browse one of the best record stores in LA? It's here at Permanent Records (see p. 90). Want to try the latest in craft beer? It's here at Eagle Rock Brewery Public House (see p. 94). What about food trucks and outdoor cinema combined? Yep, it's here at Street Food Cinema (see p. 89). Pedestrian-friendly York Street and Figueroa Street in Highland Park each lend themselves to a day's worth of wandering. Check out the boutiques, bookstores and galleries before taking to the lanes for a bowl at Highland Park Bowl (see p. 88). Likewise, add Colorado Boulevard in Eagle Rock to your tour diary for a day's exploration and for some of LA's best tacos at Cacao Mexicatessen (see p. 92).

This precinct is hip, laid-back LA, and a great option to base yourself if you're looking for a more village-like atmosphere where walking is not frowned upon. Plus, when you do crave the big smoke, it's good to know it's just a 15-minute drive or a trip on the Metro Gold Line to Downtown.

→ Googie architecture signs are still everywhere in LA

SIGHTS
1. Highland Park Bowl
2. Street Food Cinema

SHOPPING
3. Permanent Records
4. Owl Bureau

EATING
5. Cacao Mexicatessen
6. Triple Beam Pizza

EATING & DRINKING
7. Eagle Rock Brewery Public House
8. HomeState

Cindy's COFFEE SHOP

OPEN

RESTAURANT

eaks

cken

1 HIGHLAND PARK BOWL

5621 N Figueroa St,
Highland Park
323 257 2695
Mon–Fri 5pm–2am,
Sat–Sun 11am–2am
[MAP p.155 B3]

Reserve a lane, don their stylish bowling shoes and get ready to hear the crash of pins at Highland Park Bowl, a stunningly restored 1920's bowling alley. Here, 100-year-old bowling league banners and other period art cover the walls but the amenities are all 21st century. Each lane has its own comfortable couch by a large coffee table that'll become your destination for excellent food and drinks delivered by a server. In between the occasional strike, you can chow on delicious pizza, a top-quality burger and other American dishes washed down with craft beers and soft drinks. Even if you don't get a strike, you'll dig this historic local attraction.

POCKET TIP

A nature reserve in the middle of LA? You bet, Debs Park is located just south of Highland Park. More than 140 species of birds have been recorded there.

2 STREET FOOD CINEMA

Eagle Rock Rec Park
1100 Eagle Vista Dr, Eagle Rock
323 908 0607
Mon–Sun 5.30–11pm
[MAP p. 155 B1]

With its wide, open spaces and clear weather, Los Angeles has to be the perfect city for an outdoor cinema. Although Street Food Cinema pops up at various locations in LA, one of the best venues is Eagle Rock Recreation Park, a tree-lined community park with barbecue pits, sports grounds and a dog-park. Street Food Cinema shows a range of classic movies from *Star Wars* to *Grease*, with an accent on the family-friendly. Just loll back on a comfortable patch of lawn and you'll be greeted by a big screen, great sound, a bar, music and an unbeatable range of LA's favourite food trucks, such as **Tokyo Doggie Style** (Japanese fusion), **Pico House** (poke bowls) and **Burger Monster** (monster burgers).

POCKET TIP

Keep your eye out for the Richard Neutra-designed mid-century Recreation Centre, itself a local landmark that has been declared a Historic–Cultural Monument by the city.

3 PERMANENT RECORDS

5123 1/2 York Blvd,
Highland Park
323 739 0591
Mon–Sun 12pm–8pm
[MAP p. 155 B2]

Los Angeles is studded with great neighbourhood record stores but Permanent Records, on Highland Park's pumping York Boulevard strip, is easily one of the best. Permanent stocks an eclectic range of both new and used vinyl, with an eye for the outer edges of rock, soul, jazz, blues and avant-garde music. The 'Yes We're High' open sign (their closed sign reads 'Sorry We're Drunk') on the front door is a good indication of how laid-back this place is. You'll find bargains on used records and an interesting selection of the latest LPs, including a section dedicated to local artists. Don't be afraid to grab that cheap copy of Duran Duran's 'Rio' in the racks because Permanent lacks the snobbery that a lot of LA record stores suffer from. They'll always greet you here with a chill vibe.

POCKET TIP

Vintage fashions, homewares, vinyl records and well-curated fashion for men and women abound in Highland Park. Start by strolling Figueroa Street and then head over a couple of blocks to York Boulevard.

4 OWL BUREAU

5634 N Figueroa St,
Highland Park
424 285 5517
Mon–Sun 11am–7pm
[MAP p.155 B3

When owner of ad agency Chandelier Creative, Richard Christiansen, couldn't get his hands on a copy of *French Vogue* within a 45-minute drive of his home, he knew he had to do something about it. Enter bookstore, Owl Bureau in the heart of Highland Park, where design and fashion-lovers can browse the incredible collection of new and vintage books and magazines, and stay to enjoy the design of the store itself. The ornately carved owl door at the back of the room pays homage to the store's former life, as Owl Drugstore. Peruse new-release tomes, as well as collectibles from Madonna's *Sex* to 1960s copies of *Holiday* magazine displayed on custom-carved shelves made from blonde California wood. The green lab-coated staff are more welcoming than judgy (no one likes judgy). Check online (www.chandeliercreative.com/space/Owl%20Bureau) for exhibitions, book events and artists-in-residence.

POCKET TIP

Chicken Boy is a bizarre six-metre rooster-headed statue rescued from the demolition of a 1960s restaurant, that resides on top of the Future Studios Gallery on Figueroa. He's now an Instagram superstar.

5 CACAO MEXICATE**JJ**EN

1576 Colorado Blvd, Eagle Rock
323 478 2791
Tues–Thurs 11.30am–3pm
& 5–9pm, Fri 11.30am–
10pm, Sat 8.30am–10pm,
Sun 8.30am–8pm
[MAP p. 155 B1]

It's true, the ratio of incredible tacos in Los Angeles is high but there are certainly standouts and this one deserves special mention. Its duck carnitas taco wrapped in a handmade organic tortilla is cooked in its own fat and then topped with radishes, pickled red onions and salsa macha and has drawn praise from some of the world's leading food critics. Don't stop at this though, try Chef Christy Lujan's Nieman ranch pork belly chicharrones, and Santa Barbara sea urchin tostaditas. There are weekday lunch specials with drinks and sides from $11.95. Come hungry. Also noteworthy is the Mexican-focused winelist and endless coffee infused with cinnamon. The vibe here is laid-back with three different seating areas. Best is the al fresco-style out the front.

POCKET TIP

There actually is an Eagle Rock, and it is named for the eagle-shaped structure on one face of the rock. See if you can spot the outstretched wings on the Eagle Rock Canyon Walk, a 1.5 kilometre (one mile) easy loop trail.

POCKET TIP
Pair your pizza with a nice glass of organic wine at Highland Park Wine next door, which is connected to Triple Beam.

6 TRIPLE BEAM PIZZA

5918 N Figueroa St,
Highland Park
323 545 3534
Sun–Thurs 12pm–10pm,
Fri–Sat 12pm–11pm
[MAP p. 155 B3]

Who said well-known chef-produced fare has to be expensive? At this pizza joint, you pay by the weight of the slice, served Roman-style, at room temperature. Start with the margherita and then move into more experimental territory by sampling the patate pizza with fontina, potatoes and black truffle cheese or a slice of shaved asparagus with ricotta pizza pie. The crust is suitably thin and crispy. Triple Beam is a genius idea from Nancy Silverton, one of the most admired chefs in America, and Matt Molina, the James Beard winner, the award given to America's best chefs. Indoor/outdoor patio seating is casual and there's free sparkling water, too.

7 EAGLE ROCK BREWERY PUBLIC HOUSE

1627 Colorado Blvd, Eagle Rock
323 739 0081
Mon, Wed & Thurs 11am–10pm, Fri 11am–11pm, Sat 10am–11pm, Sun 10am–10pm
[MAP p. 155 B1]

Being a craft beer enthusiast can have its drawbacks; not everyone you travel with will enjoy standing in a tap room tasting flights of beer. Eagle Rock Brewery Public House addresses this by not only being a tasting room for their nearby brewery but also a destination for fine food and a good range of old and new world wines. The menu is focused on classy versions of American favourites, along with a range of vegetarian offerings and a cheese plate curated by **Milkfarm**: a local artisanal cheese store. The brewery itself has been a local go-to for over a decade and is co-owned by Ting Su, one of the first female brewers on the scene. It offers unique takes on American and European beers, including the much-heralded Yearling: a sour ale aged in Cabernet barrels.

POCKET TIP
Cruising around Highland Park and got a thirst? Drop into Galco's Old World Grocery on York who specialise in soda pop with over 400 different varieties.

8 HOME/TATE

5611 N. Figueroa St,
Highland Park
323 204 9397
Mon–Sun 8am–10pm
[MAP p. 155 B3]

Wandering down the eminently strollable Figueroa Street you may stumble across this little oasis of Tex-Mex cuisine amongst myriad boutiques and cafes. HomeState features a kid- and dog-friendly beer garden with plenty of seats; it's a choice spot for a break from retail therapy. It opens from breakfast, serving Texas border favourites such as Frito pie, migas and Texas toast along with tacos, splendid guacamole and a delightfully light kale salad. The drinks list is simple but features good quality European wine and local beers, along with cocktails and soft drinks. There's a queue to order but once you're through it's easy to find a table and chill, do some people watching and bask in the sun. Don't be surprised if that quick bite turns into a long afternoon hang.

PASADENA

Just 10 minutes' drive from Downtown, the fresh air and open spaces (plus abundant free parking) of Pasadena feels a million miles away. Think grand buildings and wide genteel boulevards, where orange trees lend a citrus aroma to the air and jacaranda blooms come out in June. It's old-school grandeur framed by the San Gabriel Mountains. Why such grandeur? Back in the 1880s Pasadena became a winter resort for wealthy sunseekers from the East Coast. Grand hotels were built including The Raymond (*see* p. 105), built in 1886. There's also an impressive range of Craftsman-style homes scattered throughout the precinct.

Renowned for the annual Rose Bowl football game, and the flower-covered floats in the New Years' Rose Bowl Parade, Pasadena is worth a visit any time of year. First stop has to be The Huntington (*see* p. 98), a verdant garden, art museum and library where you can spend a whole day exploring. Old Town Pasadena is spread across 21 blocks and offers great shopping but for real bargain hunters, best are the flea markets (*see* p. 101).

Getting around is easy. There are six Gold Line Metro stations in Pasadena originating from Downtown.

→ *The cactus-filled Desert Garden at The Huntington*

SIGHTS
1. The Huntington Library, Art Museum and Botanical Gardens
2. Echo Mountain Hike
3. The Ice House

SHOPPING
4. PCC Flea Market/Rose Bowl Flea Market
5. Simply Fresh

EATING
6. Fosselman's Ice Cream Co.
7. Julienne

DRINKING
8. 1886 Bar at The Raymond

1 THE HUNTINGTON LIBRARY, ART MUSEUM AND BOTANICAL GARDENS

1151 Oxford Rd, San Marino
626 405 2100
Wed–Mon 10am–5pm
[MAP p.167 A3]

The Huntington Library, Art Museum and Botanical Gardens in San Marino is a spectacular place. It features more than a dozen principal gardens, including the **Rose Garden**, the **Japanese Garden** and the incredible succulent and cactus-filled **Desert Garden**. There's also an **Australian Garden**. After a wander through the gardens check out the **Art Museum**, where temporary and ongoing exhibitions are held across five galleries. Be sure to visit **The Huntington Library** where there's a permanent exhibition showcasing 150 rare objects from the collection including a 15th-century manuscript of Geoffrey Chaucer's *Canterbury Tales* and documents from Abraham Lincoln's life. Time your visit with **high tea**, featuring the Huntington signature blend (with roses) and lashings of cream and jam on freshly baked scones.

POCKET TIP
There's also a new Education and Visitor Centre on The Huntington grounds and possibly the best gift shop in California.

2 ECHO MOUNTAIN HIKE

3302 Lake Ave, Altadena
[MAP p. 168 A3]

Named as one of the USA's best hikes, the Echo Mountain trail high above Pasadena offers a great workout, with incredible views of the city, wildlife and some local history. Starting at the **Sam Merrill Trail** just at the top of Altadena, the last suburb before the mountains, you ascend through scrubland until you hit the **Echo Mountain Trail** about four kilometres into the walk. It's here that you follow the trail towards the mountain summit. In the 1900s, the summit was home to a casino and hotel serviced by a light railroad, which was a popular attraction until it burned to the ground. Remnants of the railroad and hotel are still visible and there's information plaques at the summit with pictures of the old resort, along with picnic benches for a well-deserved rest. At the rear as you overlook the valley you'll find the echo phone; apparently if you yell into it you can be heard all the way across the valley at Inspiration Point. The 8.6 kilometre (5.4 miles) walk takes around two hours. Along the winding dirt track you'll spy other keen hikers, it can be a hard slog so a medium-level of fitness is required.

99

3 THE ICE HOUSE

24 N Mentor Ave
626 577 1894
Tues–Sat 6pm–2am,
Sun 5–11pm
[MAP p. 166 C2]

When comedian (and podcaster) Marc Maron wants to try out new material, this is where he goes and what's more it only costs $20 to see him do his set. Opened in 1960, this former cold storage plant (hence the name) is renowned in comedian circles as being one of the best rooms in Los Angeles, and intimate, too – with just 200 seats in the main room. Photographs of big names (Jerry Seinfeld, Steve Martin, Ellen Degeneres, Chris Rock) that have performed here line the walls. There are two showrooms and an outdoor courtyard to enjoy a drink between shows. Pricing for shows vary, for the best value go to one of their 'best of' line-ups featuring four to six comedians. Book ahead online. There is a two-drink minimum and there's food service as well; **Comics Restaurant** is open Friday and Saturday.

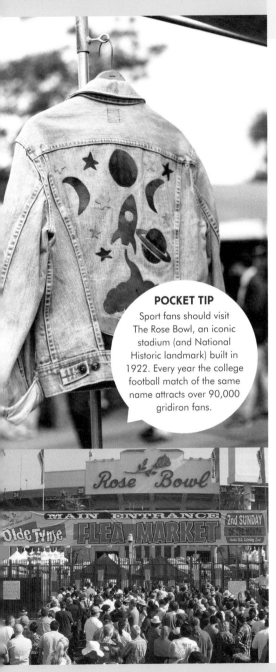

4 PCC FLEA MARKET/ROSE BOWL FLEA MARKET

Pasadena City College (PCC),
1570 E Colorado Blvd
1st Sun each month, 8am–3pm
Rose Bowl Stadium, 1001 Rose
Bowl Dr
2nd Sun each month, 7am–3pm
[MAP p. 167 A1]

The Pasadena City College (PCC) Flea Market not only has one of the best records fairs (with 50 vinyl vendors!) in town, but also hosts 400 other dealers hawking a huge array of vintage furniture, clothes and knick-knacks on the grounds and in a multi-level car park. But that's not all vintage fans! Then there's the venerable Rose Bowl Flea Market; a monster vintage fair featuring 2500 dealers that has been running continuously for 50 years. If you want a bargain, turn up early as up to 20,000 antique and vintage fashion buffs visit the fair every month. Each of the flea markets has a good selection of food vendors. There are cash machines on site, too.

POCKET TIP
Sport fans should visit The Rose Bowl, an iconic stadium (and National Historic landmark) built in 1922. Every year the college football match of the same name attracts over 90,000 gridiron fans.

5 SIMPLY FRESH

2628 Mission St, San Marino
626 441 7250
Mon 10.30am–5.30pm,
Tues 11am–5.30pm,
Wed–Sat 10.30am–5.30pm
[MAP p. 166 C4]

This is not just any lifestyle
concept store. With four
separate rooms, and an outdoor
area to peruse, Simply Fresh
is a veritable museum of gifts.
From soaps, organic baby
clothes by the likes of Milkbarn
Kids and classy California-
centric goods to jewellery,
this is the place to head for
presents for friends back home,
or a small memento of your trip.
There's also a curated selection
of books, as well as cards and a
range of themed gifts for new
babies, brides-to-be, as well as
gifts for him. And no need to
haul those shopping bags far,
as there's ample street parking
out the front of this ivy-covered
store. No wheels? Get off at the
Asuza/Citrus stop on the Metro
Gold Line and take the 176 bus
from Mission/Meridian.

POCKET TIP
Mt Wilson Observatory
sits in the snow-capped
mountains above
Pasadena and is open to
the public. This working
observatory offers an
incredible panoramic
view of the city.

6 FOSSELMAN'S ICE CREAM CO.

1824 W Main St, Alhambra
626 282 6533
Mon–Sat 10am–10pm,
Sun 11.30am–10pm
[MAP p.147 F3]

No matter where you are in LA, if you have a hankering for ice-cream, head here. An institution in Alhambra, which is just south of Pasadena, the multitude of flavours as well as the original malt-shop decor, including an original soda fountain for malts and floats, make this worth the trek. This is Willy Wonka-style territory. Fosselman's has been doing what they do for 100 years and what they do is pretty damn good. Forty flavours of hand-churned ice-cream, sorbet, soft serve, as well as malts, splits, soda fountain specialities and killer candy by the scoop. The ice-cream is superbly creamy and the chocolate malt milkshake is pure bliss. It also offers a range of ice-cream and ice-cream cakes to take away.

7 JULIENNE

2651 Mission St, San Marino
626 441 2299
Mon–Fri 8am–6.30pm,
Sat 8am–5pm
[MAP p. 166 C4]

Vases of fresh flowers and gas lanterns adorn the room at this French-inspired bistro, a local favourite for 30 years. The elegant decor takes you to the south of France, and the menu is French-inspired California fresh. Open only for breakfast and lunch, daily specials include the likes of grilled swordfish topped with roasted pineapple salsa or mango chicken salad, and come with a glass of wine. Julienne is also great for people-watching. On the outdoor patio Pasadena's finest discuss the latest local goings-on while sipping wine and forking salads, their hair immaculate, their linens freshly pressed.

POCKET TIP
Head next door to Julienne's take-away market where there's a selection of breads, pastries and conserves.

POCKET TIP

The downtown business district of Old Pasadena was founded in the late 1800s. It has been reinvigorated whilst retaining its old-world charm. Head for Fair Oaks Avenue and dine and shop in one of the best shopping districts in Southern California.

8 1886 BAR AT THE RAYMOND

1250 S Fair Oaks Ave
626 441 3136
Tues–Thurs 11.30am–12am,
Fri–Sat 11.30am–2am,
Sun 11.30am–12am
[MAP p. 166 B3]

A haven for cocktail enthusiasts who prefer their libations made with freshly squeezed juice and adorned with hand-cut block ice, the 1886 Bar successfully blends two essentials in a good drinking establishment: incredible cocktails and great ambience. It's a relaxed, cosy bar with press-tinned ceilings, tufted leather furniture and original wood accents. The name represents the first incarnation of the historic Raymond Hotel before a fire ravaged through in 1895. The bar, which opened in 2010, is known for its range of off-menu concoctions. If your preferred cocktail is not on the menu they can make it for you with a repertoire of 600 recipes. If you're not sure what you want, ask for a 'dealer's choice' where the bartender can whip up the perfect drink to your preferred tastes. Their happy hour goes from 4–6pm (Tues–Fri) where select cocktails are $7 and wines $5.

THE VALLEY

Just 'over the hill' from Hollywood and Beverly Hills, The Valley (officially The San Fernando Valley) is quintessential California. Encompassing the area from the Santa Monica Mountains to the Verdugo mountains to the east, the Valley is the setting for movies we grew up on, from *Fast Times at Ridgemont High* to *Boogie Nights*, and from *E.T.* to *The Karate Kid*. Not surprising really, the movie and TV studios are situated here, and if you're in LA for the magic of movies, you must set aside time to do the Warner Bros. Studio Tour (see p. 108). Beyond the studios is a sprawling metropolis filled with shopping malls, bowling alleys, neon signs, motels and carwashes (you can get a good sense of this at the Valley Relics Museum, see p. 110).

If you want a real retro California experience head to this precinct, there's also an array of incredible restaurants and bars, such as Smoke House (see p. 117) and Tonga Hut (see p. 116). Hire that convertible you've always dreamt about (you'll need the fresh breeze, it's around 10 degrees Celsius hotter in the Valley), over that 'hill' is a journey well worth taking.

California car culture is big here but it's good to know there are public transport options including the $8 FlyAway service (see p. 140) from LAX to Van Nuys Airport which gets you close to the action and the Metro Red Line which stops in North Hollywood (a misnomer, it's way north, in the Valley) and Universal City from Downtown Los Angeles.

→ *The giant neon clown in North Hollywood has long been a San Fernando Valley beacon*

SIGHTS
1. Warner Bros. Studio Tour
2. Moonlight Rollerway
3. Valley Relics Museum

SHOPPING
4. It's A Wrap
5. MIDCENTURYLA

EATING
6. Petit Trois
7. Guisados

DRINKING
8. Tonga Hut
9. Smoke House

1 WARNER BROS. STUDIO TOUR

3400 Warner Blvd, Burbank
818 977 8687
Mon–Sun 8.30am–3.30pm
[MAP p. 162 C3]

There are other studio tours in Los Angeles but what makes the Warner Bros. Studio tour so great is that it's a working set with some of the top TV shows with 35 sound stages and 14 exterior sets right here. The *Ellen DeGeneres Show* is being filmed as you walk through, so is *Conan* (which is worth booking online for free tickets). On the tour you'll be able to visit the sets of big hits like *The Big Bang Theory* and even sit down and pretend you're drinking coffee at Central Perk (from *Friends*). Films are being made too, who knows who you might bump into at the Warner Bros. Commissary Dining Room. You'll also get to see costumes, sets and memorabilia from past hits like the *Harry Potter* and *Batman* films, as well as the street scenes from *Casablanca*.

POCKET TIP

Want to drive by *The Brady Bunch* home? (Recently revived by home renovation TV show *HGTV*). Head to 11222 Dilling Street North Hollywood and try to stop the flood of memories.

2 MOONLIGHT ROLLERWAY

5110 San Fernando Rd, Glendale
818 241 3630
Mon–Sat 1.30–4pm, 8–11pm,
Sun 1.30–4pm, 7.30–10pm
[MAP p. 163 F3]

Rollerskating (as an adult) always sounds good in theory. In reality, when the skates are strapped on and those wheels are the only thing separating your fragile body with that hard, hard floor, it can be terrifying. Unless you go to Moonlight Rollerway. Any fears of falling will be allayed simply because you are having so much fun. They love a themed night here, Wednesday night is Rainbow skate night for LGBTIQ+ skaters, expect dancing and divas on the tracklist; and on Tuesday, an 86-year-old, the Fabulous Dominic, plays Hammond organ, the last of the roller-skating rink organists in California. Oh, and look out for actor John C. Reilly who has been known to skate here alone, he's a big fan.

3 VALLEY RELICS MUSEUM

7900 Balboa Blvd, Lake Balboa
818 616 4083
Thurs–Sat 11am–4pm,
Sun 11am–3pm
[MAP p.164 B2]

Not so much a museum as a neon, pop-culture wonderland; this giant warehouse features mid-century neon signs, fast food packaging, television ephemera and other remnants of mid-century Valley life. Most of it comes from the collection of Tommy Gelinas, who is the founder and head curator of the Valley Relics. You enter via a small museum shop (they have a great selection of T-shirts) and admission is $10; Valley Relics is a non-profit organisation and all proceeds go towards acquiring and preserving artefacts reflecting the cultural history of the San Fernando Valley. There's the bull-horned Pontiac Bonneville owned by famed cowboy fashionista Nudie Cohn, the sticker covered door from Jan Brady's room in *The Brady Bunch* and neon signs from long-vanished Valley icons like the Palomino and Outrigger. Best of all? That row of pinball and video game machines are free to play.

POCKET TIP
Check out the nearby 94th Aero Squadron restaurant. It's on the runway at Van Nuys airport, they offer headphones with your meal, so you can listen in to air traffic control.

4 IT'S A WRAP

3315 W Magnolia Blvd,
Burbank
818 567 7366
Mon–Fri 10am–8pm,
Sat–Sun 11am–6pm
[MAP p. 162 C2]

This is a vintage clothing store with a difference, much of the stock is sourced from working studio sets, so you could be wearing Rachel from *Friends'* 501s or more realistically, shows that we know but weren't major hits like *New Girl* (two racks worth). Because it's renowned for stocking garments from Tinseltown, this place is full of shoppers. There's always a queue of people lining up to ravage the racks directly after you. The best approach? Elbows out! Rummage through those Hollywood wardrobes (and props too) but be prepared to put in the hard yards, there's a lot to get through, and those racks are packed tight. Celebrity seconds needn't come at a premium, there's bargains to be had, check the racks outside the front door for clothes from $1.

POCKET TIP

Take some time to cruise down Ventura Boulevard in nearby Sherman Oaks, a vibrant shopping strip chock full of new and vintage boutiques, quirky shops and good food.

111

5 MIDCENTURYLA

5333 Cahuenga Blvd,
North Hollywood
818 509 3050
Mon–Sun 10am–5pm
[MAP p. 162 B2]

Serious furniture and homewares lovers make this giant warehouse their first stop when in Los Angeles. When TV set designers were shopping for the fabulously vintage hit series *Mad Men*, they came here. Why? Owner David Pierce has a great eye for sourcing pieces from Scandinavia, Germany, Holland and Belgium, and what's more, they're reasonably priced. Think clean-lines from the likes of Hans Wegner, Finn Juhl and Arne Jacobsen. Go in for a peek at this veritable design museum, the place is packed to the ceiling full of the good stuff. There are smaller pieces for sale that fit easily into a suitcase like ceramics and servingware, plus artworks.

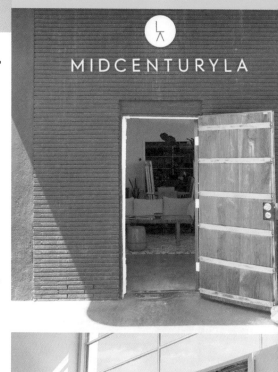

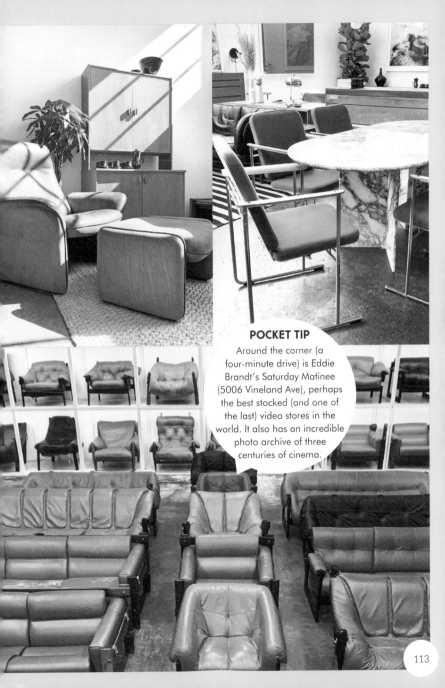

POCKET TIP

Around the corner (a four-minute drive) is Eddie Brandt's Saturday Matinee (5006 Vineland Ave), perhaps the best stocked (and one of the last) video stores in the world. It also has an incredible photo archive of three centuries of cinema.

113

6 PETIT TROI*

13705 Ventura Blvd,
Sherman Oaks
818 989 2600
Mon–Sun 8am–10pm
[MAP p. 165 B3]

There comes a point in any visit to the US when you simply can't stomach another burger or hot dog; you've done the tacos, the sushi and the salads, you need something else. Enter Petit Trois, a modern French bistro that has a great reputation, and it's not just because of the marble bar, the minty banquettes and the black and white tiled floor, making you feel like you're in Paris. It's for the steak tartare, the bouillabaisse, and special mention must go to the Omelette Petit Trois, a fluffy folded combination of eggs, boursin pepper cheese and chives. Leave some space for the Tahitian vanilla bean crème brûlée, too. If you're not sure which French wine to choose, the sommelier will make recommendations in an unsnooty manner. Merci to that, and a tout de suite!

7 GUISADOS

312 N San Fernando Blvd,
Burbank
818 238 9806
Mon–Thurs 9am–10pm, Fri–Sat
9am–11pm, Sun 9am–9pm
[MAP p. 163 D2]

This family run taqueria first
opened on the eastside in
Boyle Heights, and proved so
popular they've added a few
more including this indoor/
outdoor Burbank post on the
main shopping street. What
makes their tacos some of
the best in LA? The fillings
are braised for hours (guisado
means braises/stews) and their
corn tortillas are freshly made.
LA's famous food critic, the late
Jonathan Gold once declared
their chiles toreados to be a
'natural phenomenon'. This
habanero, serrano, jalapeno
and Thai chilli with beans
taco comes with a warning
of its extreme spiciness
(any adjustments are kindly
declined). Be sure to order the
quesadilla, a thick chunk of
queso fresco inside a tortilla
coated with chipotle sour
cream, and an agua frescas to
wash it down. The vibe here
is chilled, a colourful mural
occupies one wall indoors but
it's best to sit out the front and
enjoy the view.

8 TONGA HUT

12808 Victory Blvd, Burbank
818 769 0708
Mon–Sun 4pm–2am
[MAP p. 165 C2]

It's dark, really dark, but as your eyes adjust to the light you find yourself ensconced amongst bamboo-lined walls and booths, tiki ornaments, fake waterfalls and bottles upon bottles of rum behind a long, well-patroned bar. Tonga Hut is LA's oldest Tiki Bar (opened in 1958 and restored to its original jungle room splendour in 2005) and the atmosphere is very authentic with exotica music on the stereo and patrons wearing tiki staples such as Hawaiian shirts and even the occasional fez. There's a storage case for personal tiki mugs owned by locals who take their tiki drinks very seriously. Rum takes centre stage here with a cocktail list that includes classics like Mai Tais and Zombies, along with house specialties such as the coconut and rum wallop of voodoo juice.

9 SMOKE HOUSE

4420 W Lakeside Dr, Burbank
818 845 3731
Mon–Thurs 11.30am–10pm,
Fri–Sat 11.30am–10.30pm,
Sun 9am–8.30pm
[MAP p. 162 C3]

Word has it that after filming
E.R. at Warner Brothers
studios, George Clooney would
head across the road and take a
seat at one of the semi-circular
red banquettes at Smoke
House. There must be some
truth to this rumour because
Clooney named his company
'Smoke House Productions',
an ode to this classic bar and
restaurant. This is also the
lounge where Ryan Gosling's
character plays the piano in *La
La Land*. Come here for happy
hour (20 per cent off Mon–Sat
4–7pm & Sun 3.15-5pm) and
sip a dirty martini and eat the
famous garlic bread. Here, the
lights are dim, wood panelling
abounds and the atmosphere
is decidedly old-school. If
you're lucky you might see a
performance by Jimmy Angel,
a former classmate of Elvis'
who sports a wig like The
King's pompadour. Having a
drink here means you're in
good company indeed.

DISNEYLAND

No matter what your age, when in LA, at least one visit to Disneyland Resort is mandatory. Most of us grew up with Mickey, Donald or the Pixar crew (to name just a few) so it makes sense we'd be curious to see just how magic the real-life experience really is.

Be warned though, the 'Happiest Place on Earth' can easily turn into the Most Frustrating Place on Earth if you don't plan ahead. Two words: the queues! First things first, the map might say Disneyland in Anaheim is just east of LA but it can take a good chunk out of the day driving there and back, so it's best to stay the night or even two in Anaheim. Disney Resort has three themed hotels onsite and there are many hotels in the area. There are shuttle services from LAX available, and the Pacific Surfliner train will take you to Anaheim station, which is a 45-minute walk to Disney. If you buy a two-day Hopper ticket you'll get entry to Disneyland and the adjacent California Adventure Park, which is as good as Disneyland.

You also need to get wise to the free Fastpass, a system that allows you to pre-book a time within a one-hour window to experience individual rides on the most popular attractions at Disneyland and California Adventure Park. The easiest way is to purchase the Disney MaxPass feature, so you can make Disney Fastpass selections directly from your phone using their app (there's free wi-fi in select areas of the park mapped in the app). It's also advisable to grab some lunch outside the peak munching hours to avoid queues and secure a table. Okay, now we've got the formalities out of the way, let's have some fun. See disneyland.disney.go.com for more information.

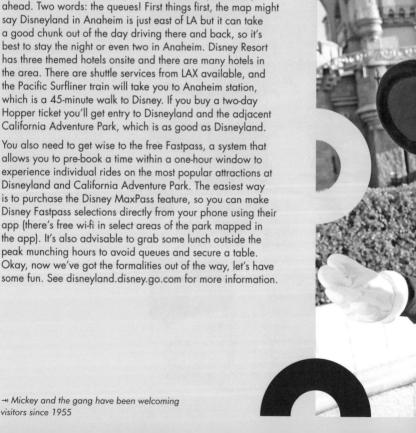

→ *Mickey and the gang have been welcoming visitors since 1955*

POCKET TIP

The food offerings have improved in the past couple of years (no longer just fat and sugar). Check out the tiki-themed Tropical Hideaway in Adventureland with good vegetarian options.

NEWER RIDES

There's always something new at California's Disneyland Resort and often the newest rides are the most popular. Take the new **Star Wars: Galaxy's Edge**, at more than 5.5 hectares (13.5 acres), it's the largest single-themed land in Disney Park's history. One of the highlights here is **The Millennium Falcon**, the 'fastest hunk of junk in the galaxy', where you'll be strapped into the Falcon cockpit and get to take the controls as pilots, gunners or flight engineers on a mission to deliver smuggled goods. It's well worth the wait.

Also recent is the newly revamped **Pixar Pier** at California Adventure Park, where you can mosey on over to a classic carousel starring Jessie the Yodelling Cowgirl. Here you will see all the faves, including characters from *Toy Story*, *Monsters, Inc.* and *Cars*.

THE CLASSICS

But let's not forget the old classic rides, including **It's A Small World**, a psychedelic boat ride (don't drink the water!) musical diorama of all the nations of the world, and **Indiana Jones Adventure** – a bone-jarring jeep ride with great special effects. There's also **The Haunted Mansion**, where a steady stream of 'Doom Buggies' carry the brave through spooky rooms full of poltergeists.

For thrillseekers, line up for the indoor rollercoaster, **Space Mountain** and next door at California Adventure Park there's the **Guardians of the Galaxy: Mission Breakout**, an unnerving sudden drop and quick ascent in a dark lift shaft. Equally scary is the **Incredicoaster** rollercoaster at California Adventure Park, with its catapult start and circle motions.

There's musicals to watch such as *Frozen* and *Tale of the Lion King* and characters to meet for photo opportunities and autographs.

POCKET TIP
Be sure to stick around for the nightly Electrical Parade down Main Street USA featuring 600,000 lights, as well as the fireworks.

121

PALM SPRINGS

For a glorious period in the mid 20th century, Palm Springs was an oasis embodying the good life. This is where Hollywood glamour lolled poolside, when movie studios had a contract clause that their biggest signings couldn't be further than two hours away from Los Angeles (around 100 miles) in case they were needed for a studio lunch or a photo shoot. Stroll any street and you were likely to see the swinging-est people gathering for cocktail hour. Names such as Elvis Presley, Bing Crosby, Frank Sinatra, Dean Martin and Sammy Davis Jr. In those days, the stars took their pleasure seriously.

Now, in part thanks to the Coachella music festival in April and the revival of mid-century architectural design, Palm Springs – a two-hour drive east of LA – is enjoying its day in the sun again. The LA hip set flock here for weekends spent poolside against the backdrop of the San Jacinto Mountains in hotels or in mid-century modern masterpieces. And a new breed of celebs have now arrived to enjoy the good life (and the architecture), with stars like Leonardo DiCaprio moving in. You too can experience the glamour by visiting the mid-century Honeymoon Hideaway (*see* p. 124), where Elvis and Priscilla Presley honeymooned, or stay at the fabulously retro Parker Palm Springs (*see* p. 127).

One thing to note: it gets hot here, really hot, so firey you can't even sit at your poolside cabana from mid-morning through to mid-afternoon, so check the forecast if you're travelling in summer. Driving is the best option both to get to Palm Springs and to get around the town.

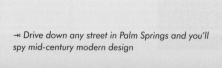

→ *Drive down any street in Palm Springs and you'll spy mid-century modern design*

POCKET TIP

Get a bird's-eye view of the desert by going on the Palm Springs Aerial Tramway. It's the world's largest rotating tram car.

DESIGN

See some of the glorious mid-century homes for yourself by pulling up outside Elvis' **Honeymoon Hideaway** (1350 Ladera Circle) where The King whisked new bride Priscilla back in 1967. Known as the 'House of Tomorrow', it was designed by prolific modernist architect William Krisel. You can tour the house, sit on the giant curved banquette sofa and even peek at the marital bed.

If you're feeling flush, you can choose to stay at **Frank's house** (1145 E Vía Colusa). Sinatra led the pack (and the rats duly followed) in 1946 by hiring architect E. Stewart Williams to design his house complete with a heated, piano-shaped swimming pool. They say the chip on the bathroom sink is from Ol' Blue Eyes throwing a bottle in a rage.

ЅHOPPING

If you want to take home a slice of mid-century, the **Uptown Design District** (along North Palm Canyon from Vista Chino to Alejo) is full of galleries, antique malls and consignment stores. Highlights here include **Iconic Atomic** (1103 N Palm Canyon Dr) for vintage Aloha shirts and tiki paraphernalia and **Shag the Store** (745 N Palm Canyon Dr) for fine art by the celebrated mid-century artist Shag (aka Josh Agle).

Prefer a bargain? If you walk into the **Angel View** thrift store (462 N Indian Canyon Dr) and browse through its 'prestige' collection, you'll see racks of pristine chinchilla stoles, rows of newly pressed leisure suits, gabardine slacks and cabana wear. Perfect for living the Palm Springs' life!

125

POCKET TIP

Palm Springs is quite the
festival town year-round
with The Palm Springs
International Film Festival,
Modernism Week and Palm
Springs Pride bringing the
biggest crowds.

EATING & DRINKING

It's the desert so the theory
might be that fresh food is
hard to come by. Not so at
Farm (6 La Plaza), a restaurant
tucked away in a plaza where
you can sit out in the French-
inspired garden patio and feast
on fresh salads (try the roasted
pear salad), sandwiches and
crepes. Oh, and they do the
best coffee in town too.

The **Amigo Room** at the
Ace Hotel & Swim Club
(701 E Palm Canyon Dr) is
a good choice for a drink,
they offer artisanal cocktails
and a wide selection of craft
beers. The space is cool (in
both senses of the word) and
there's a decent diner onsite
called **King's Highway** if
you need a burger break.
There's also a photo booth
to record your Palm Springs'
visit in a nostalgic sort of
way! The bar often hosts live
events, including bands, DJs
and comedy and is the party
destination for **Coachella**
in April and **Gay Pride** in
October/November.

/LEEPING

You're going to want to stay for a night or two, and there's a bounty of mid-century hotels to choose from, as well as holiday homes for rent. My choice? The 144-room **Parker Palm Springs** (4200 E Palm Canyon Dr), where hammocks are slung between palm trees, there's a fire-pit for late-night chats and in between dips in one of the three pools, you can enjoy a spot of croquet, tennis or petanque. They do good mid-week rates off-season. A word of warning: while the restaurant, Mister Parker's is beautifully designed, prices can be quite steep.

Another great mid-century option is the **Del Marcos Hotel** (225 W Baristo Rd), designed and built in 1947 by William F. Cody. After lounging poolside you might want to make use of their free bike hire to discover some of the city's dazzling history and architecture.

LOS ALAMOS

Once just a restroom stop off Highway 101, Los Alamos has become California's coolest culinary destination. Lately, a new restaurant or bar is opening monthly on the main street of this tiny town (population 1800) near the Santa Ynez Valley, a 45-minute drive north-west of Santa Barbara (and a two-and-a-half-hour drive from Los Angeles). Former Los Angeles high-flying entertainment executives and actors have carved out a new life pursuing their passion for the region's organic produce here. You can have a drink at actor Kurt Russell's The Wine Saloon (*see* p. 132) or possibly the best pain au chocolat in the US at Bob's Well Bread Bakery (*see* p. 130), which is run by a former Sony executive.

The town has a main street that looks like it is straight out of a Wild West movie set and is surrounded by ranches, farms and vineyards. Los Alamos may be small but there's definitely a long weekend's worth of food and fun to be enjoyed here.

The Pacific Coast Highway drive is a must to experience, with the glorious ocean on one side and clifftop mansions, roadside restaurants and galleries (the Getty Villa for one) on the other. Once you get from LA to the Spanish-styled city of Santa Barbara then it's time to head inland. The best way to get here is to drive, or you can take a bus (five and a half hours) via Santa Maria.

→ *Old west architecture dominates in Los Alamos*

POCKET TIP

En route from LA to Santa Barbara, stop at La Super-Rica Taqueria (622 N Milpas St) for fish tacos. It was one of Julia Child's favourites and Angelenos have been known to go there just for their lunchtime taco fix.

LOS ALAMOS FOUNDED 1876

EATING

Begin your stay with a bakery treat at **Bob's Well Bread Bakery** (550 Bell St). When Bob Oswaks wanted a change of pace from his intense Hollywood role running the marketing for Sony Pictures Television he turned to organic bread making. The passion became a full-time pursuit when Bob transformed a former filling station into an artisanal bakery making breads in small batches in a custom-built, stone-deck oven. Here baguettes and croissants abound, as do delicious kouign-amann (a Breton cake) and canelé. They also serve Stumptown coffee, which could be the best brew on the West Coast.

Keeping with the bready theme, **Full of Life Flatbread** (225 W Bell S) serves organic flatbread pizza using local seasonal ingredients. Their Central Coast Sausage pizza featuring naturally raised pork, blue agave and fennel sausage is every bit as tasty as it sounds. For dessert, cooks place giant bubbling marshmallow s'mores in the 20-ton stone beehive oven, it's an over-the-top gooey sensation. Come early, lines can be long.

DRINKING

Journalist-turned-winemaker Sonja Magdevski's **Tasting Room** (388 Bell St) together with the adjoining **Babi's Beer Emporium** (named after her grandmother), is the perfect entrée to a night out on Bell Street. Sonja's **Casa Dumetz Wines** focus on small production Rhône varietals crafted on the foundation of Santa Barbara County fruit. Be sure to try the viognier. The rooms get packed when Sonja hosts a regular guest series.

Head for a nightcap at **The Wine Saloon** (362 Bell St) – a historic saloon – complete with swinging doors – where the owner is none other than actor Kurt Russell. You might not see Kurt slinging drinks but his sister Jami Way will entertain with stories of the bar's history. Johnny Cash is said to have played in this room, which is full of taxidermied beasts and chandeliers that were used in the movie *Gone With the Wind*. Keeping it in the family, Jami serves wines from Kurt and Goldie Hawn's GoGi wine estate.

POCKET TIP

Next door to The Alamo is the huge Depot antique mall where you can pick up vinyl to spin on the portable record player in your room.

SLEEPING

It's a small town, but Los Alamos lays claim to two of California's coolest (and inexpensive) motels. Once a run-down hacienda-style motel (think beige walls and floral bedspreads), **The Alamo Motel** (425 Bell St) has been reinvented by motelier group Shelter Social Club. The style is minimalist rustic featuring artworks by local creatives. On site is the **Municipal Winemakers**' tasting hut, serving wine made by David Potter who trained in Australia.

Up the road, and up a hill is the newly renovated **Skyview Motel** (9150 US-101). It too has gone with the rustic-chic look and offers a full-service restaurant, heated pool, plus a working vineyard.

JOSHUA TREE

There's something otherworldly about Joshua Tree National Park. Peering across the desert sunset among Joshua trees and yuccas, it's easy to see why artists, musicians and writers decamp here, sometimes for good.

The national park just off Twentynine Palms Highway is full of life. Mormon tea, juniper, jack rabbits and coyotes bide their time in the heat amongst the rugged rock formations. Lizards and sidewinder rattlesnakes sunbake and slink along the hot sand. Hiking trails abound, save them for sunrise and sunset, and bring water. With little light pollution, the stargazing here is also some of the best in the US. And the name Twentynine Palms? Legend has it that the name of Twentynine Palms was first used by gold miners because of the 29 Washingtonia filifera palm trees surrounding the Oasis of Mara in the town of Joshua Tree, the area was once a favourite camping spot for Native Americans.

Driving is the best way to get to Joshua Tree, any public transport also involves a (rather hefty) taxi ride. It's a three-hour drive east of Los Angeles so best to stay for a night or two. The journey to Joshua Tree is a seemingly endless highway where fast food joints and strip malls eventually make way for giant windmill fields, bringing energy to the desert.

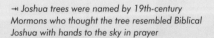

→ *Joshua trees were named by 19th-century Mormons who thought the tree resembled Biblical Joshua with hands to the sky in prayer*

/IGHT/

Joshua Tree Cultural Expeditions (www.boxoprojects.com/cultural-expeditions) offers tours of the cultural landscape of Joshua Tree National Park and the surrounding area, including an outdoor art foundation, an arts residency, an art compound and unique architecture of the **Harrison House** and the **Kellogg Joshua Tree House**. The latter is an otherworldly structure made of 26 cantilevered concrete columns set into the natural bedrock. If you're not taking the tour, you can visit the house but you have to book an event there. A visit to **The Integratron** can also be organised through Joshua Tree Cultural Expeditions – it's a unique soundbath where quartz crystal bowls are played live in a dome-shaped room. Be prepared for an experience.

HIKING

Of course, any trip to Joshua Tree will involve as much time spent as possible exploring the national park. Winter, spring and autumn (fall) are best for hiking; and sunset and sunrise are the best times of the day to see wildlife, and view the incredible colours of the rocks against the changing hues of the sky. There are numerous easy loop hikes, including the two kilometre (1.3 miles) **Barker Dam** hike, which takes you past wildflowers, rocks, Joshua trees and the dam. The more challenging **Ryan Mountain** hike, at 4.8 kilometres (three miles) affords an incredible view atop the peak. Be sure to also take a walk around the 1.6 kilometre (one mile) **Cap Rock** loop and along the way there are signs placed giving hikers information on the desert. You'll also see a shrine here to musician Gram Parsons. Parsons was a member of The Byrds and The Flying Burrito Brothers in the 1960s, he died in 1973 in a motel room in Joshua Tree and, honouring a pact the two made, his tour manager took his body and set it alight at Cap Rock (there's a movie about it starring Johnny Knoxville called *Grand Theft Parsons*). Maps for all hikes are available at: www.nps.gov/jotr/planyourvisit/maps.htm

SHOPPING, EATING & DRINKING

In Yucca Valley, **The End** (55872 Twentynine Palms Hwy) sells vintage fashions. Even if you don't buy anything you can admire the murals that cover the exterior of the shop, hand-painted by owner and artist Kime Buzzelli and Los Angeles artist Elena Stonaker. At **BKB Ceramics** (61705 Twentynine Palms Hwy) you can pick up beautifully handcrafted pots, as well as jewellery.

For breakfast, fuel up before your hike by heading to **Crossroads Cafe** (61715 Twentynine Palms Hwy), where they offer creative spins on diner classics, including good vegan options. Try the tofu scramble.

After a long day exploring, pull up a bar stool or grab a booth at the **Joshua Tree Saloon** (61835 Twentynine Palms Hwy) right by the entrance to Joshua Tree National Park. It's the sort of place where you can hear tall tales over a beer and burger.

NIGHTLIFE & SLEEPING

For great music, venture to **Pappy and Harriet's** in nearby Pioneertown (53688 Pioneertown Rd). It's a honky tonk where top bands play (think Ariel Pink and The Oh Sees), just check out their calendar online. They also do a great barbecue, all their organic meats and fish are cooked on their outdoor grill with Mesquite Wood. Try the ribs.

The **Joshua Tree Inn** (61259 Twentynine Palms Hwy) is nice enough as roadside inns go, with a pool, a pergola and free breakfast. It's infamous for being the place where aforementioned singer Gram Parsons died back in 1973 at just age 26. Many, including U2, who named an album after the desert, have stopped by to pay respects.

Prefer something a little more rustic? **JT Homesteader Cabins** offer three semi-off-grid dwellings in the Coyote Valley, available on Airbnb. Two cabins have power, water and wi-fi; and for the more adventurous, one has only water and a small solar charger for a mobile phone. All three are Instagram sensations.

GETTING TO LO/ ANGELE/

International flights arrive at **Los Angeles International Airport** (LAX). A whopping 85 million air-travel passengers pass through this airport each year, and the good news is that to accommodate this growing number, it's undergoing a massive renovation until 2023. If you're lucky enough to arrive or depart at the **Tom Bradley International Terminal** you can get an idea of the new look: it's roomier, there's a good selection of shops and restaurants and an abundance of electrical outlets for charging devices. All of LAX has free wi-fi too. (*See* www.flylax.com)

There are new rules for taxis and ride-share pick-up services such as **Uber/Lyft** services at LAX, which were recently introduced due to congestion. You will need to catch a free shuttle bus from your terminal to the nearby LAX-it (pronounced LA Exit) pickup lot. Shuttles arrive every five minutes. Just outside the terminal, the LAX-it lot is also walkable, it's right next to Terminal 1 and it's an 8-minute walk from Terminals 2, 7 and 8. (*See* www.flylax/lax-it)

LAX FlyAway buses (lawa.org/flyaway) offer regularly scheduled round-trip services from LAX terminals to Van Nuys, Union Station, Westwood, Hollywood, and Long Beach. Get tickets online; $8 to $10 one way.

Domestic flights also arrive and depart at the following airports:

Hollywood Burbank Airport (BUR)

If you're arriving in LA on an internal flight and staying in the Valley, consider landing at Burbank's less-crowded, commonly called Bob Hope Airport, which is serviced by most major US airlines including Delta and United. (*See* hollywoodburbankairport.com)

Long Beach Airport (LGB)

Long Beach Airport has taxi stands outside the terminal. Ride-share services are available on the outer curb in front of the terminal. The closest Metro rail station is Wardlow Station on the Blue Line. A fare to here from the airport is around $13.50. (*See* www.lgb.org)

GETTING AROUND LO/ ANGELE/

Los Angeles is a spread out megalopolis, but once you get your bearings it's relatively easy to navigate (though a map always helps); think ocean to the west and mountains to the north.

Rush hour is not limited to one hour in the morning and afternoon, it runs from 6am to 10am and then again from 3pm to 7pm. And on Fridays? Forget about it – it's all day.

Walking

Unlike what you might have seen in movies and TV, LA does have definite precincts, like West Hollywood or Silver Lake and Los Feliz, which make walking a good option.

Don't jaywalk, heavy fines can be enforced.

Metro

There's good public transportation with the mostly above ground **Los Angeles Metro** train, as well as Uber and Lyft ride-share. The Metro (www.metro.net) offers six fast rail lines to as far out as Long Beach, The Valley and Pasadena.

A handy way of planning your route is to use the Metro Trip Planner (socaltransport. org/tm_pub_start.php), which gives detailed instructions on how to get to and from your destination. All transit rates start at a base fare of $1.75. Another option is the Metro Day Pass ($7) and the 7-Day Pass ($25). Buy your tap on/tap off tickets at Metro stations.

Buses

There are over 165 bus routes serving the county of Los Angeles. You can buy tickets with cash onboard, though you must have exact change (see Metro rates above) or use the **Metro Tap** card.

Local buses are painted orange, they stop around every two blocks. Rapid buses do fewers stops, they are painted red. Express buses travel on freeways for longer distances and have a higher premium, and Orange and Silver Lines are Bus Rapid Transit lines (BRT) that run on dedicated busways. Timetables and maps are available at: www. metro.net

Driving

It has to be said, there is a certain pleasure in making a California-centric mixtape (*see* p. 144 for suggestions) and driving around LA, blue sky above, and palm trees fringing the road.

There are numerous car hire companies surrounding the airport with free shuttle services from LAX.

In the United States, traffic keeps to the right. If there are no posted signs, the maximum speed is 25 miles per hour (40 km/h) on city streets and 65 miles per hour (104km/h) on freeways. A right turn on a red light after stopping is permitted unless otherwise indicated. At a four-way stop sign intersection, right of way goes to the car that got there first (after stopping, of course).

Parking fines are easy to come by in LA, so it's good to know the rules beforehand. Read the signs carefully, and check the curb. A red curb means no parking, a green curb indicates parking for a limited time only, and a white or yellow curb indicates passenger loading and unloading.

If driving, practise defensive driving, and pay extra for the car insurance.

VISAS

International travellers come to the United States for a wide variety of reasons, including tourism, business, medical treatment and certain types of temporary work. The type of visa needed is defined by immigration law, and relates to the principal purpose of your travel.

The **Visa Waiver Program** enables most citizens or nationals of participating countries (*see* https://travel.state.gov) to travel to the United States for tourism for stays of 90 days or less without obtaining a visa. Travellers must have a valid **Electronic System for Travel Authorization** (ESTA) approval prior to travel. You need to apply for ESTA no later than 72 hours before departing for the United States. Real-time approvals are no longer available and arriving at the airport without a previously approved ESTA will likely result in being denied boarding. Always apply at the official site (below), as there are some dodgy third-party sites out there. (*See* https://esta.cbp.dhs.gov/esta/)

STATE & LOCAL TAXES

The state-wide sales tax is 7.25 per cent. Local taxes may add up to 1.5 per cent to your total bill.

TOURIST INFORMATION

The **Los Angeles Tourism & Convention Board** has information centres located at the InterContinental Los Angeles Downtown, Union Station, the San Pedro/Los Angeles Waterfront, and Hollywood & Highland. (*See* www.discoverLosAngeles.com)

LGBTIQ+

Los Angeles is home to one of the most welcoming LGBTIQ+ communities in the world, from West Hollywood, Silver Lake and Los Feliz to the beach cities and The Valley. The heart of Southern California's largest LGBTIQ+ community is in West Hollywood, site of the **Gay Pride** parade in June (lapride.org), **Halloween Costume Carnaval** on 31 Oct (www.visitwesthollywood.com/halloween-carnaval/), and **Outfest** in July (www.outfest.org). **The Abbey** (*see* p. 33) is a local icon and the most famous of WeHo's clubs and bars. Many events and nights for the LGBTIQ+ community occur weekly in a range of different venues and locations.

EVENTS

For a good round up of what's on, see:
For events: www.laist.com
For music:
www.losangeles.ohmyrockness.com
For food: www.laeater.com
Los Angeles magazine: www.lamag.com

PUBLIC HOLIDAYS

New Year's Day 1 January

Martin Luther King Jr. Day The third Monday in January

Presidents' Day The third Monday in February

Cesar Chavez Day 31 March

Memorial Day The last Monday in May

Independence Day 4 July

Labor Day The first Monday in September

Indigenous Peoples' Day The second Monday in October

Veterans Day 11 November

Thanksgiving The fourth Thursday in November

Friday after Thanksgiving The Friday following the fourth Thursday in November

Christmas 25 December

If the following dates fall upon a Saturday, the preceding Friday is a holiday: 1 January, 4 July, 11 November, 25 December.

If the following dates fall upon a Sunday, the following Monday is a holiday: 1 January, 4 July, 11 November, 25 December.

EMERGENCY

Police, Fire, Ambulance EMERGENCY Dial: 911

TIME ZONES

Los Angeles is in the Pacific Time Zone (Greenwich Mean Time minus 8 hours).

The state of California observes daylight savings time from early March through to early November.

MONEY & ATMS

All prices quoted in this book are in $USD.

Cash machines/ATMs can be found throughout all of the shopping and eating districts, inside bank branches and in petrol stations.

When withdrawing from an ATM the Los Angeles Police Department (LAPD) advise to walk purposefully with confidence and give the appearance that you are totally aware of your surroundings.

Be aware of ATM fees, it's wise to speak with your bank before leaving to find out the best way to avoid hefty international transaction fees, and to let them know you will be in the US so they can monitor any suspicious activity on your cards.

It's always good to have some US dollars on you upon arrival, especially a wad of $1 notes for tipping.

TIPPING

Tipping is customary. A gratuity charge is not automatically included in the bill at restaurants and other establishments unless it is noted on the cheque (read over it carefully!). Adding 15 to 20 per cent for restaurant and taxi service is customary, and a few dollars for an Uber or Lyft ride-share driver.

Luggage handlers are usually tipped $1 to $2 per bag. A $1 to $2 tip is customary for parking lot attendants and valets. When tipping for maid service in a hotel, $1 to $2 per day or $5 to $10 per week is a good guideline.

Getting a haircut or your nails done? Be sure to tip 15 to 20 per cent.

Buying a drink at a bar? Tip at least $1 per drink bought.

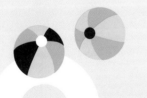

CLIMATE

Renowned for its glorious weather, Los Angeles enjoys comfortable temperatures and low humidity year-round. There's an old song about how it never rains in Southern California. It's not true, it does a tiny bit, and it's not all sunshine and blue skies. Go there in May or June and expect what's known as 'May grey' or 'June gloom'. It usually clears to blue come the afternoon, though.

Pack a bathing suit, sunscreen and light clothes (plus athletic wear for hikes) but do bring a sweater/jumper and light jacket as it can get cool at night.

Average Temperatures:

Spring (March–May): 10–25° C (50–75° F)

Summer (June–August): 15–35° C (55–90° F)

Autumn (September–November): 15–25° C (55–75° F)

Winter (December–February): 5–20° C (40–70° F)

It's generally warmer in The Valley and cooler near the beaches.

PHONES

To call Los Angeles dial the US country code +1, then the three digit area code, which varies across the city (noted in each listing) and then the number.

Domestic and international calling cards can be purchased at local convenience stores and petrol stations. Prepaid SIM cards, available from telecommunications stores such as T-Mobile and AT&T are another good option.

Or you can utilise your own mobile phone roaming, just check the rate before leaving.

WI-FI

There is no shortage of opportunities to access free wi-fi in Los Angeles. Some parks offer free wi-fi, including Griffith Observatory (*see* p. 14), Echo Park Lake and even the boardwalks of Venice Beach.

Hanging out in Beverly Hills, Downtown or Santa Monica? There's access to free wi-fi there.

Many hotels offer free wi-fi, as do department stores, museums such as LACMA (*see* p. 78) and The Hammer (*see* p. 53), as well as Los Angeles Public Library (*see* p. 63).

DRINKING

The legal drinking age in California is 21 years old.

Last call for drinks in Los Angeles is at 2am.

CANNABIS LAWS

Under California law, adults 21 or older can buy, consume, possess, and grow cannabis up to the limits set by state law. If you are 21 or older, you can buy and possess up to one ounce (28.5 grams) of cannabis and up to eight grams of concentrated cannabis.

[Source: City of Los Angeles Department of Cannabis Regulation https://cannabis.lacity.org/]

Whether you're a medical or recreational user, it remains illegal to consume cannabis in public. And never consumer cannibis before, or while driving. It's illegal to take cannibis across state lines, even to another state where cannabis is legal.

SECURITY & SAFETY

Despite seeing fires, shootouts, quakes, and any other apocalyptic events both in movies and sometimes on the news, Los Angeles is a reasonably safe city. But like any big city, you need to be aware of your surroundings and the people around you. If someone is making you uncomfortable for any reason at all, move away from them.

You will notice that sadly homelessness is a reality in Los Angeles. In 2019, L.A. County's homeless population was at 58,936. Housing affordability is the biggest factor driving homelessness. Whether you feel inclined to give money to someone asking for it is up to you. If you decline, be polite, some homeless people are mentally ill or have substance abuse issues, being rude is not advised, and could put you at unnecessary risk, plus it's uncalled for.

HEALTHCARE

Always, always get health insurance, as should anything go wrong in the US, the medical bills can be incredibly expensive, even if it's a slight injury or ailment. Before signing up to your travel insurance read the fine print to note exclusions.

VOLTAGE & CONVERTERS

Electrical current is 110 volts AC. Converters can be purchased at local pharmacies, or requested at your hotel's concierge or guest services desk, they are also available from airports.

EMBASSY CONTACTS

Australian Consulate General
2029 Century Park East, Suite 3150
Los Angeles, CA 90067
310 229 2300
www.losangeles.consulate.gov.au

New Zealand Consulate General
2425 Olympic Blvd, Suite 600E
Santa Monica, CA 90404
310 566 6555
www.mfat.govt.nz/en/countries-and-regions/north-america/united-states-of-america/new-zealand-consulate-general-los-angeles/

British Consulate General
2029 Century Park East, Suite 1350
Los Angeles, CA 90067
310 789 0031
gov.uk/world/usa

Canadian Consulate General
550 South Hope St, 9th Floor
Los Angeles, CA 90071-2627
213 346 2700
international.gc.ca/world-monde/united_states-etats_unis/los_angeles.aspx

ESSENTIAL LOS ANGELES MIXTAPE

Buy or stream these songs, wind down the windows and cruise down the California highway.
The Beach Boys – *Surf's Up*
N.W.A – *Straight Outta Compton*
Randy Newman – *I Love LA*
Guns 'N Roses – *Welcome to the Jungle*
Joni Mitchell – *California*
Flying Burrito Bros – *Sin City*
X – *Los Angeles*
Lee Moses – *California Dreamin'*
Love – *Between Clark and Hilldale*
Tupac – *California Love*
Elliott Smith – *Alameda*
Thee Midniters – *Whittier Blvd*
Black Flag – *TV Party*
Buffalo Springfield – *For What It's Worth*
Sam Cooke – *A Change is Gonna Come*
The Go-Go's – *This Town*
Bob Seger – *Hollywood Nights*

B

C

I

SAN
FERNAN

SIMI
VALLEY

164 —

165 —

THOUSAND
OAKS

ENCINO

2

CALABASAS

LOS
ANGELES

158–9 —

To NEPTUNE'S NET
(NOT SHOWN ON MAPS)
←

BOARDRIDERS
MALIBU

MALIBU

SANTA
MONICA

3

TOPANGA
BEACH

170–1 —

173

VENI

172 —

Santa
Monica
Bay

4

A

B

C

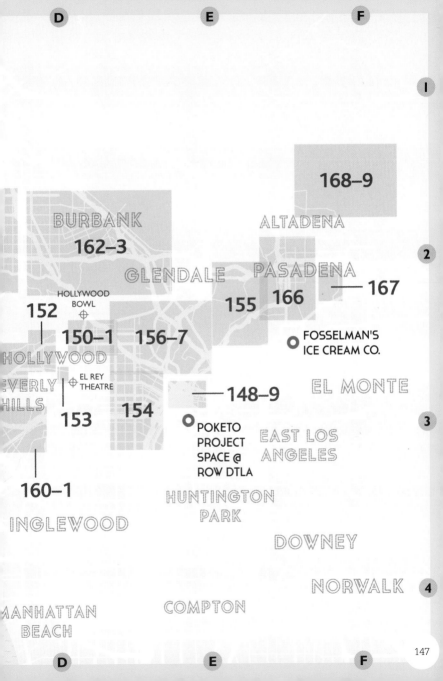

D   E   F

I

168–9

BURBANK

ALTADENA

162–3

2

GLENDALE   PASADENA

HOLLYWOOD
BOWL ⊕   **155**   **166**   — **167**

152

150–1   **156–7**

HOLLYWOOD   ○ FOSSELMAN'S
            ICE CREAM CO.

EVERLY   ⊕ EL REY
       THEATRE   EL MONTE

HILLS   — **148–9**

153   **154**

          ○ POKETO   EAST LOS   **3**
           PROJECT   ANGELES
           SPACE @
           ROW DTLA

160–1

         HUNTINGTON
         PARK

INGLEWOOD

                     DOWNEY

                        NORWALK   **4**

MANHATTAN   COMPTON
BEACH

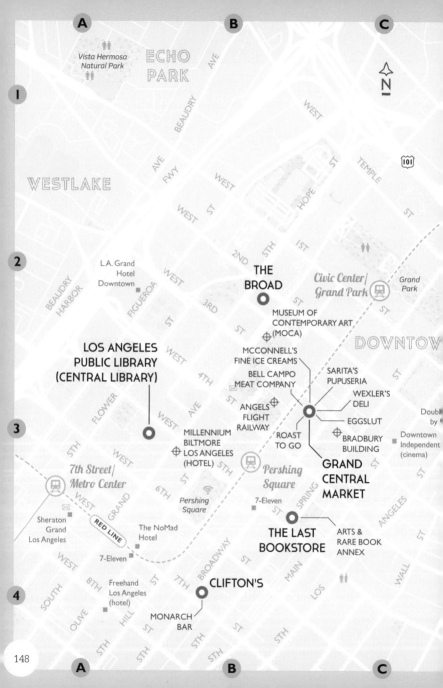

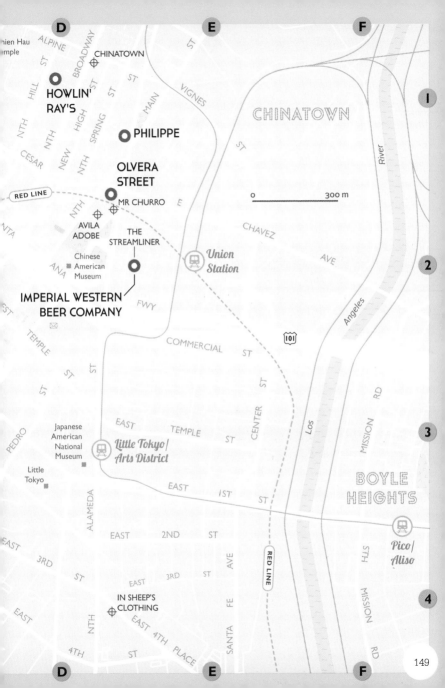

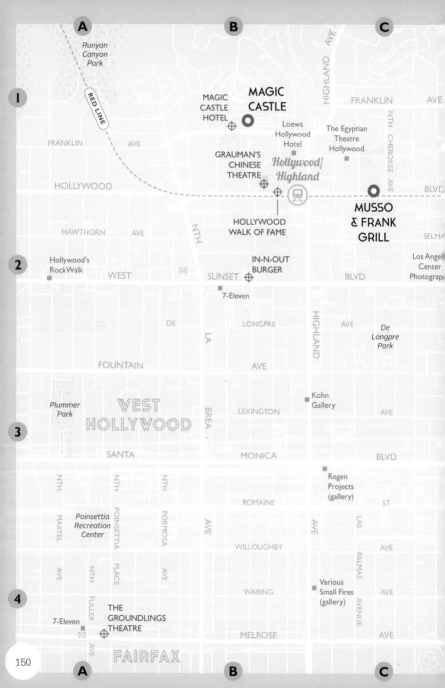

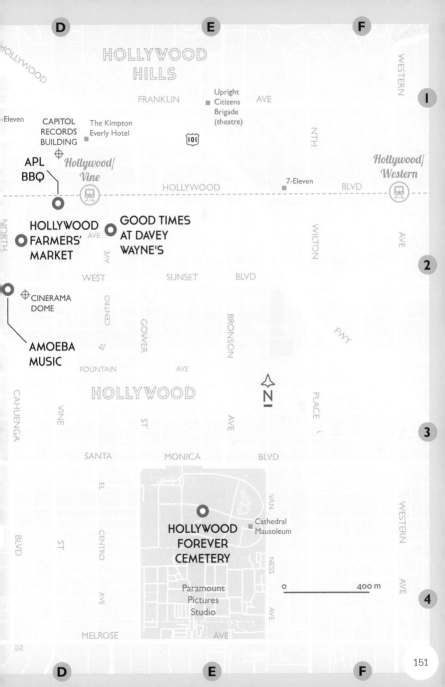

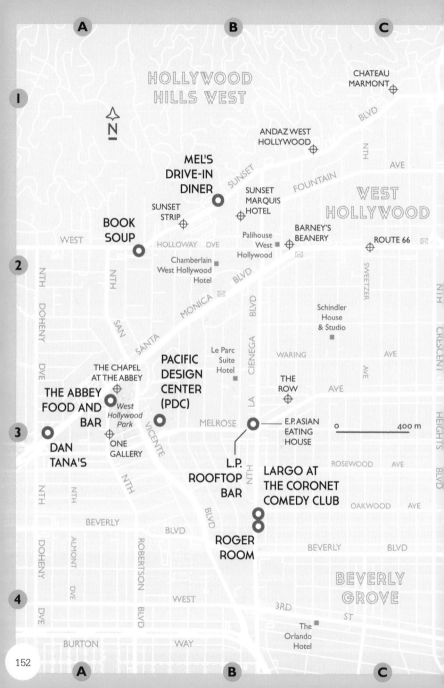

A

B

C

1

HOLLYWOOD HILLS WEST

CHATEAU MARMONT ⊕

BLVD

N

NTH AVE

ANDAZ WEST HOLLYWOOD ⊕

FOUNTAIN

WEST HOLLYWOOD

MEL'S DRIVE-IN DINER ◎

SUNSET

SUNSET MARQUIS HOTEL ⊕

SUNSET STRIP ⊕

BARNEY'S BEANERY ⊕

ROUTE 66 ⊠

WEST

BOOK SOUP ◎

HOLLOWAY DVE

Palihouse West Hollywood ■ ⊠

NTH

SWEETZER

NTH

CRESCENT

2

NTH

DOHENY

NTH

Chamberlain West Hollywood Hotel ⊠

MONICA

BLVD

Schindler House & Studio ■

SANTA

SAN

Le Parc Suite Hotel ■

WARING

AVE

AVE

HEIGHTS

THE CHAPEL AT THE ABBEY ⊕

PACIFIC DESIGN CENTER (PDC)

LA CIENEGA

THE ROW ⊕

AVE

BLVD

3

THE ABBEY FOOD AND BAR ◎

West Hollywood Park

◎

MELROSE ◎

E.P. ASIAN EATING HOUSE

0   400 m

DAN TANA'S ◎

VICENTE

ONE GALLERY ⊕

L.P. ROOFTOP BAR

NTH

LARGO AT THE CORONET COMEDY CLUB

ROSEWOOD AVE

OAKWOOD AVE

NTH

NTH

NTH

BEVERLY

BLVD

◎
◎

ROGER ROOM

BEVERLY

BLVD

BEVERLY GROVE

4

DOHENY

DVE

ALMONT

DVE

ROBERTSON

BLVD

WEST

3RD

ST

The Orlando Hotel ■

BURTON

WAY

152

A

B

C

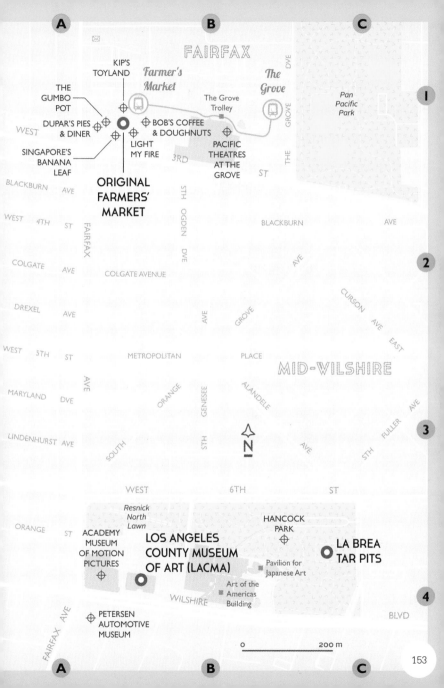

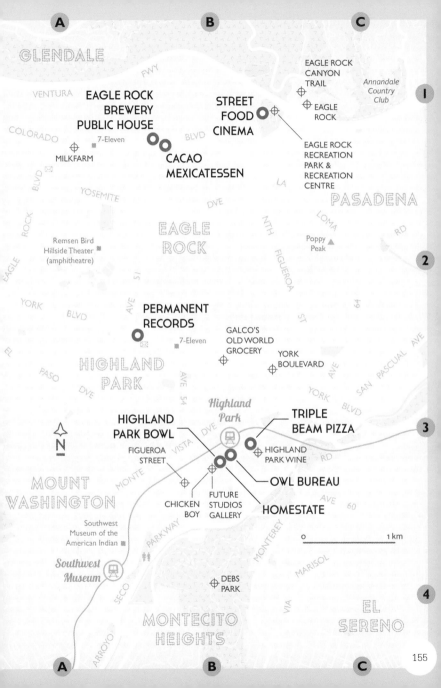

GLENDALE

A · B · C

EAGLE ROCK
CANYON TRAIL

Annandale
Country
Club

1

FWY

VENTURA

EAGLE ROCK
BREWERY
PUBLIC HOUSE

STREET
FOOD
CINEMA

EAGLE
ROCK

COLORADO

7-Eleven

BLVD

MILKFARM

CACAO
MEXICATESSEN

EAGLE ROCK
RECREATION
PARK &
RECREATION
CENTRE

PASADENA

BLVD

YOSEMITE

DVE

LA

NTH

LOMA

RD

EAGLE ROCK

ROCK

Remsen Bird
Hillside Theater
(amphitheatre)

FIGUEROA

Poppy
Peak

2

EAGLE

51
AVE

YORK

BLVD

PERMANENT
RECORDS

ST

64

SAN PASCUAL AVE

7-Eleven

GALCO'S
OLD WORLD
GROCERY

YORK
BOULEVARD

EL

PASO

DVE

HIGHLAND
PARK

54
AVE

YORK

BLVD

AVE

Highland
Park

HIGHLAND
PARK BOWL

TRIPLE
BEAM PIZZA

3

N

FIGUEROA
STREET

VISTA

DVE

MONTE

Highland
Park

HIGHLAND
PARK WINE

RD

MOUNT
WASHINGTON

CHICKEN
BOY

FUTURE
STUDIOS
GALLERY

OWL BUREAU

HOMESTATE

AVE

60

Southwest
Museum of the
American Indian

0   1 km

PARKWAY

MONTEREY

Southwest
Museum

SECO

DEBS
PARK

MARISOL

VIA

EL
SERENO

4

ARROYO

MONTECITO
HEIGHTS

A · B · C

155

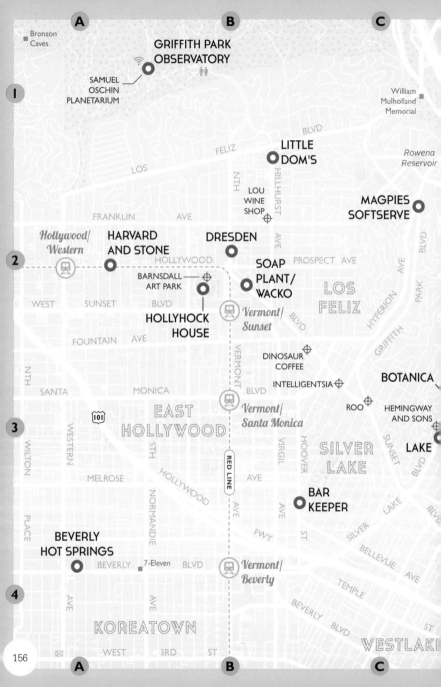

GRIFFITH PARK
OBSERVATORY

SAMUEL
OSCHIN
PLANETARIUM

Bronson
Caves

William
Mulholland
Memorial

FELIZ

BLVD

LOS

Rowena
Reservoir

LITTLE
DOM'S

LOU
WINE
SHOP

MAGPIES
SOFTSERVE

FRANKLIN   AVE

Hollywood/
Western

HARVARD
AND STONE

DRESDEN

SOAP
PLANT/
WACKO

PROSPECT AVE

HOLLYWOOD

BARNSDALL
ART PARK

HOLLYHOCK
HOUSE

Vermont/
Sunset

LOS
FELIZ

WEST   SUNSET   BLVD

FOUNTAIN   AVE

DINOSAUR
COFFEE

INTELLIGENTSIA

BOTANICA

NTH

SANTA

MONICA

Vermont/
Santa Monica

ROO

HEMINGWAY
AND SONS

LAKE

WILTON

EAST
HOLLYWOOD

101

SILVER
LAKE

WESTERN

MELROSE

RED LINE

BAR
KEEPER

PLACE

BEVERLY
HOT SPRINGS

7-Eleven   BLVD

BEVERLY

Vermont/
Beverly

KOREATOWN

WEST   3RD   ST

WESTLAKE

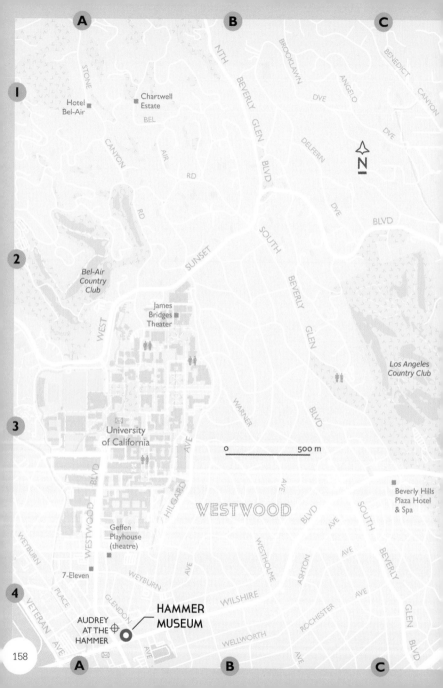

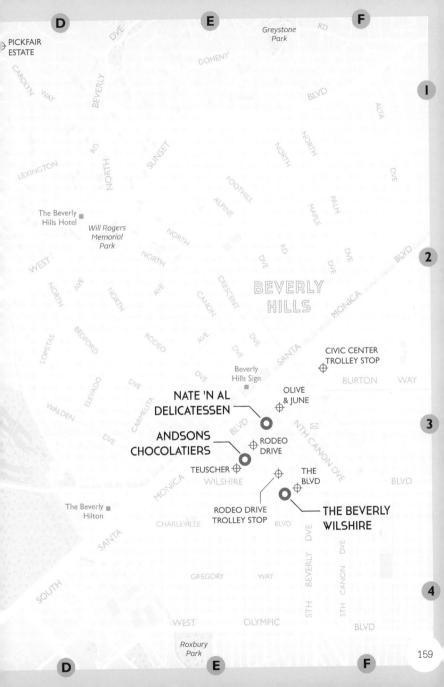

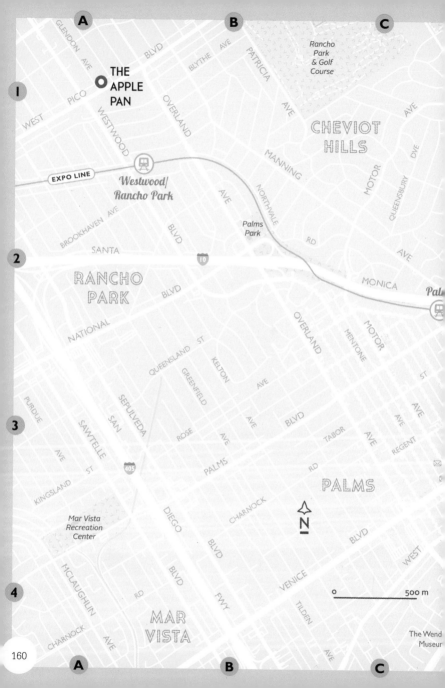

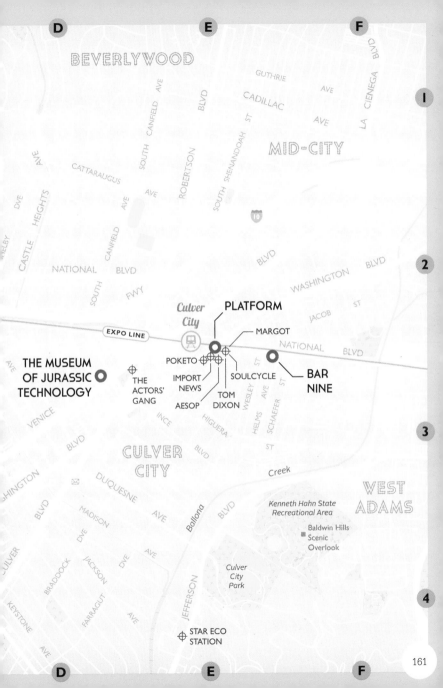

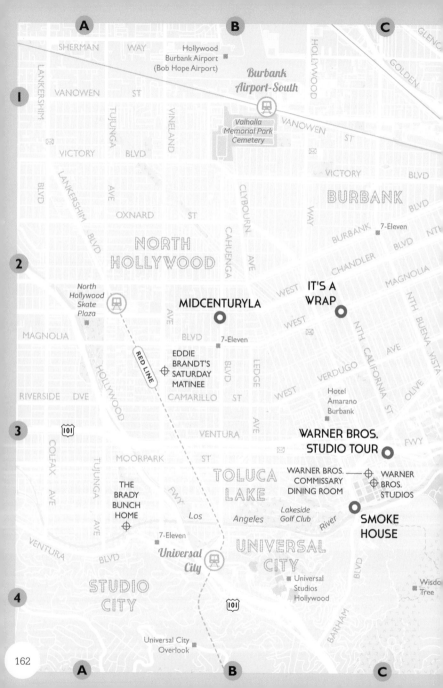

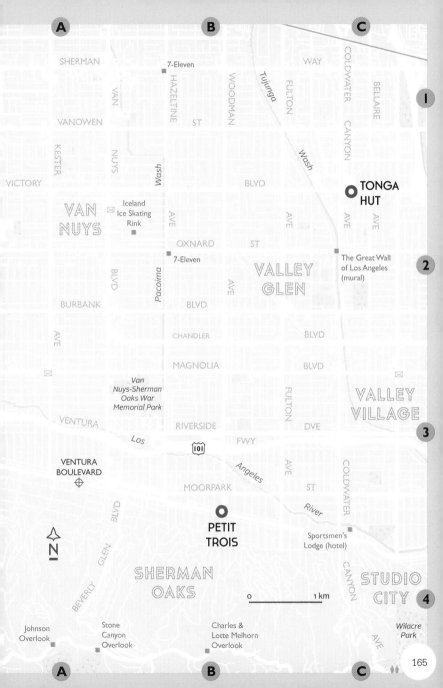

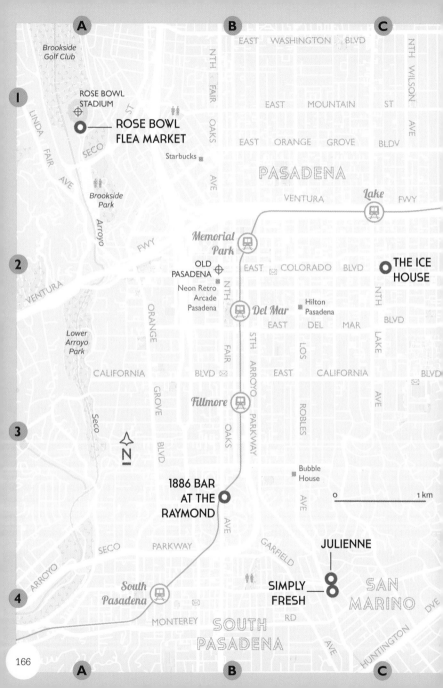

A

B

C

EAST WASHINGTON BLVD

Brookside
Golf Club

I

ROSE BOWL
STADIUM

● ROSE BOWL
FLEA MARKET

NTH FAIR OAKS ST

NTH WILSON AVE

EAST MOUNTAIN ST

EAST ORANGE GROVE BLDV

LINDA FAIR AVE

Starbucks

PASADENA

Brookside
Park

VENTURA

Lake FWY

Arroyo

FWY

2

Memorial
Park

THE ICE
HOUSE

VENTURA

OLD PASADENA

EAST COLORADO BLVD

Neon Retro
Arcade
Pasadena

Del Mar

Hilton
Pasadena

Lower
Arroyo
Park

ORANGE GROVE BLVD

EAST DEL MAR BLVD

NTH LAKE AVE

BLVD

CALIFORNIA

Seco

FAIR OAKS

NTH STH ARROYO PARKWAY

LOS ROBLES

EAST CALIFORNIA BLVD

3

Fillmore

N

1886 BAR
AT THE
RAYMOND

Bubble
House

AVE

0   1 km

JULIENNE

SECO PARKWAY

GARFIELD

SIMPLY
FRESH

SAN
MARINO

4

South
Pasadena

ARROYO

MONTEREY RD

SOUTH
PASADENA

HUNTINGTON DVE

AVE

A

B

C

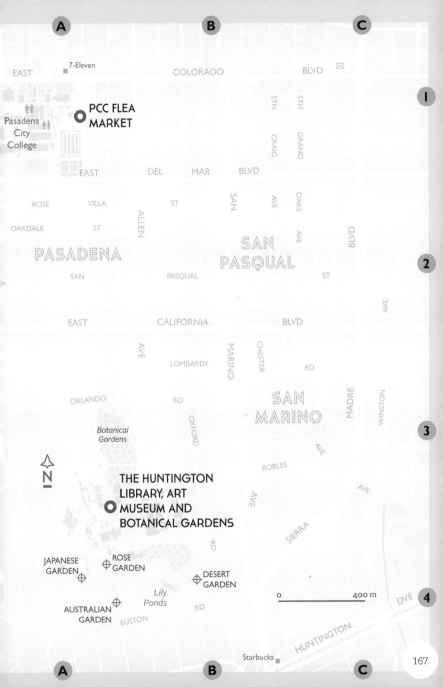

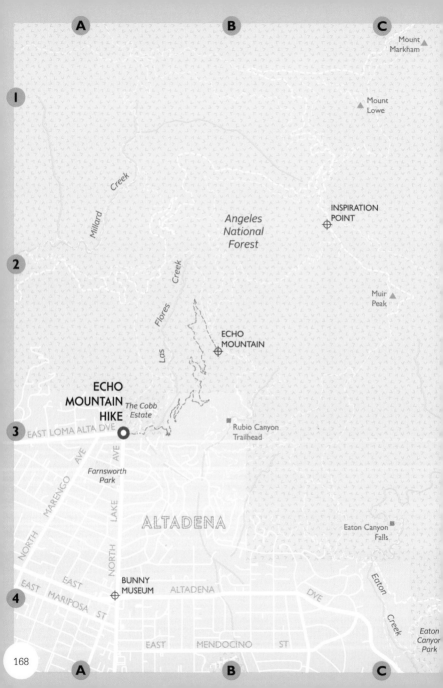

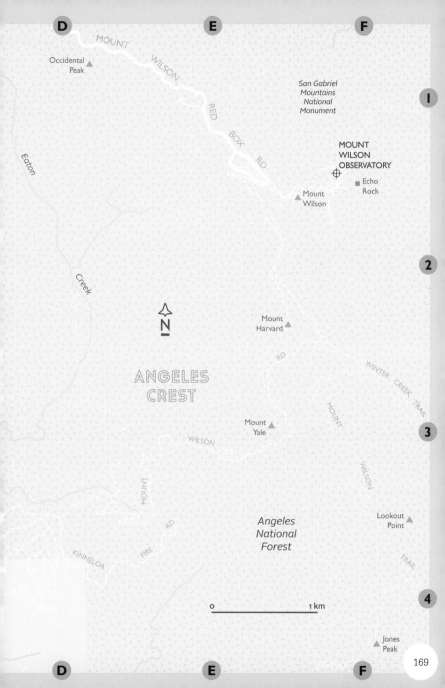

SANTA MONICA

Douglas Park

The Aero Theatre (cinema)

17th Street / Santa Monica College

Miles Memorial Playhouse (theatre)

Oceana Beach Club Hotel

SIDECAR DOUGHNUTS & COFFEE

7-Eleven

Eli and Edythe Broad Stage (theatre)

The Cove Skate Park

FAIRMONT MIRAMAR HOTEL & BUNGALOWS

GLAM+GO

BIKE CENTER GUIDED TOUR

HOTEL SHANGRI-LA SANTA MONICA

Woodlawn Cemetery

ONYX ROOFTOP LOUNGE

EXPO LINE

Downtown Santa Monica

Santa Monica State Beach

CAMERA OBSCURA ART LAB

THE BIKE CENTER SANTA MONICA

7-Eleven

Le Meridien Delfina Santa Monica

SANTA MONICA PIER

Original Muscle Beach

0   500 m

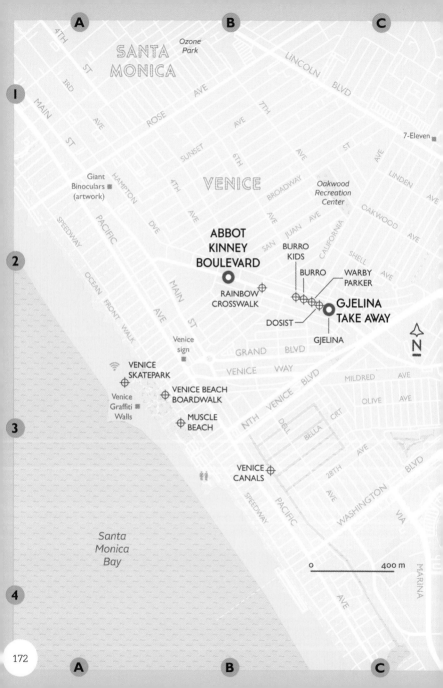

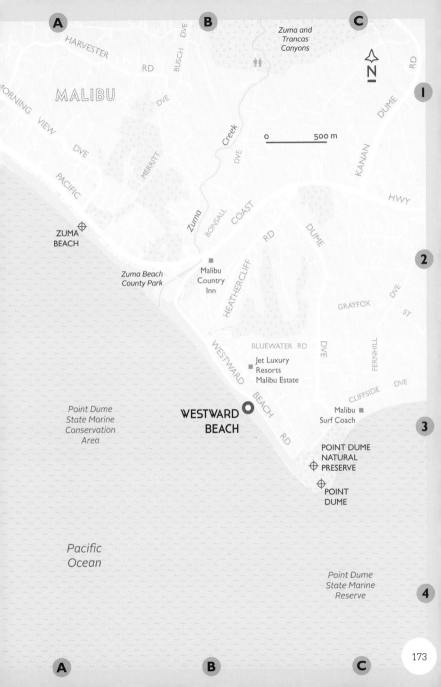

INDEX

ABOUT THE AUTHOR

Australian freelance writer and editor, Andrea Black has been a regular visitor to Los Angeles since she was a child. In the past 15 years she has spent quality time every year exploring the city. At first, she found the sprawling city overwhelming but has since discovered the key to this metropolis: exploring one precinct at a time. Specialising in travel writing as it relates to design, architecture and music, Andrea's work has been published in magazines and newspapers from *The New York Times Magazine* to *Better Homes and Gardens*. She regularly contributes to *Traveller* in the *Sydney Morning Herald*, the *Age*, *The Weekend Australian* and *Escape*. She worked as an editor of magazines before going freelance, giving her more time to visit Los Angeles and discover new precincts of this endlessly fascinating city.

ACKNOWLEDGEMENTƧ

It was the music of Los Angeles that first got me; from Gram Parsons to West Coast hip hop and Southern California soul. Then it was the architecture, the mid-century design bringing the outside in. And what an outside it is; blue skies and mountainous nature walks amongst the urban sprawl.

Now I love Los Angeles mostly for the great Angeleno friends I have made. Thanks to Tracy, Marnie, Alex and Tom, Geoffrey and Barrie for all the suggestions and your good company whilst visiting various establishments across the city. Extra special thanks to my husband Russell for exploring it all with me, helping with the research and taking all the shots along the way. I couldn't have done it without you.

Thank you to Melissa Kayser and Megan Cuthbert at Hardie Grant, and project editor Alice Barker for all the hard work and incredible encouragement. And to Michelle Mackintosh and Megan Ellis for their design and typeset.

PHOTO CREDIT/

All images are © Andrea Black except for the following contributed images:

Jennifer Chong pg. i; Marissa Vitale pg. ii, 42, 43 (top; middle left; middle right), 45 (top and bottom); Tawny Alipoon pg. iv (top left); Santa Monica Travel & Tourism pg. iv (top centre); Little Dom's pg. iv (top right), 20, 21 (top); Christian Rocchi pg. iv (middle left); Zach Bresnick pg. iv (middle centre); Poketo pg. iv (middle right), 66, 67, 177 (lower middle); Parker Palm Springs pg. iv (bottom left); Ed Rudolph pg. iv (bottom centre); Botanica pg. iv (bottom right), 22, 23 (top right), 23 (middle left; bottom right); Travis Conklin pg. vi; Discover Los Angeles pg. 1; Hollywood Forever Inc; pg. 3 (middle and bottom); Esotouric pg. 4; Discover Los Angeles pg. 5 (top); Nancy Rodriguez pg. 6 (top and bottom); Magic Castle pg. 7 (top); Tina Whatcott Echeverria pg.8; Jakob Layman pg. 9; Luke Gibson pg. 10; Luke Gibson pg. 11; Discover Los Angeles pg. 12; Griffith Observatory pg.14 (top); Joshua White Photography pg. 15; Melissa Klages pg. 16; Jennifer Chong pg. 19; Gentland Hyers pg. 23 (top left); Zebulon pg. 24; Ryan Forbes pg. 26; Russell Gearheat pg. 29 (middle and bottom); Ryan Forbes pg. 30 (top); Discover Los Angeles pg. 31 (middle), 36, 39 (top), 60, 64 (middle), 68 (top; middle), 77 (bottom); Dan Tana's pg. 32; The Abbey Food and Bar pg. 33; Christian Rocchi pg. 34 (top and bottom); Jen J Photography pg. 34 (middle); The Roger Room pg. 35; Santa Monica Travel and Tourism pg. 38; Shutterstock pg. 40, 41; Boardriders Malibu pg. 44; Tawny Alipoon pg. 47; Onyx Bar pg. 48, 49; Beverly Wilshire pg. 52; Elon Schoenholz pg. 53 (bottom); Ed Rudolph pg. 55 (top); Chris Dibble pg. 55 (bottom); Platform pg. 56; Bar Nine pg. 59; Visit California pg.63, 64 (top), 78 (top), 106, 139 (bottom); WonHo Frank Lee pg. 72; Clifton's pg. 73 (bottom); The Line Hotel pg. 74; Museum Associates; LACMA pg. 78 (bottom); Museum Associates; LACMA pg. 79; Beverly Hot Springs pg. 80; The Original Farmer's Market pg. 81 (top); Oriana Koren pg. 84 (top); Dylan + Jeni pg. 84 (bottom); Jenn Emerling pg. 85 (top); Oriana Koren pg. 85 (bottom left and right); Danielle Bernabe pg. 88 (top and bottom); Wonho Frank Lee pg. 88 (middle); Street Food Cinema pg. 89; David Benjamin Sherry pg. 91; Eagle Rock Brewery pg. 94; Jakob Layman pg. 95 (top); Home State pg. 95 (middle and bottom); The Huntington Library Art Collections and Botanical Gardens pg. 98; Visit Pasadena pg. 99 (top), 101; Liana's Workshop pg. 100; Acuna Hansen pg. 105; Warner Bros pg. 108 (top); Discover Los Angeles pg. 108 (bottom); Moonlight Rollerway pg. 109 (bottom); MidcenturyLA pg. 112 (bottom), 113; Petit Trois pg. 114; The Smoke House pg. 117; Disney pg. 118, 120, 121; Palm Springs Tourism pg. 122, 124, 125 (top; bottom), 126; G Aleman pg. 126 (bottom); Parker Palm Springs pg. 127; Tenley Fohl pg. 130; Visit Greater Palm Springs pg. 131, 132 (top), 135, 138, 139 (top); Zach Bresnick pg. 132 (bottom); Shelter Social Club pg. 133 (top); Zach Bresnick pg. 133 (bottom); Miles McGuinness pg. 136 (top); [JOSHUA TREE] AGENCY PIC pg. 136 (bottom); [JOSHUA TREE] AGENCY PICS pg. 137; Home State pg. 176 (upper middle); Ed Rudolph pg. 176 (lower middle); Eagle Rock Brewery pg. 176 (bottom); Platform pg. 177 (top); Bar Nine pg. 177 (upper middle); Eagle Rock Brewery pg. 177 (bottom).

POCKET PRECINCT/ /ERIE/

Curated guidebooks offering the best cultural, eating and drinking spots to experience the city as the locals do. Each guidebook includes detailed maps at the back and a field trip section encouraging you to venture further afield.

COLLECT THE /ET!

These compact guides are perfect for slipping into your back
pocket before you head out on your next adventure.

COMING /OON

Published in 2020 by Hardie Grant Travel,
a division of Hardie Grant Publishing

Hardie Grant Travel (Melbourne)
Building 1, 658 Church Street
Richmond, Victoria 3121

Hardie Grant Travel (Sydney)
Level 7, 45 Jones Street
Ultimo, NSW 2007

www.hardiegrant.com/au/travel

A catalogue record for this
book is available from the
National Library of Australia

Los Angeles Pocket Precincts
ISBN 9781741176803

10 9 8 7 6 5 4 3 2 1

Publisher
Melissa Kayser

Project editor
Megan Cuthbert

Editor
Alice Barker

Trainee editor
Jessica Smith

Proofreader
Rosanna Dutson

Cartographer
Jason Sankovic and
Emily Maffei

**Cartographic
research**
Claire Johnston

Design
Michelle Mackintosh

Typesetting
Megan Ellis

Index
Max McMaster

Prepress
Megan Ellis and
Splitting Image Colour
Studio

Printed in Singapore by 1010 Printing
International Limited